BELL JAR
BUTTERFLY

BELL JAR
Butterfly

A FAMILY'S MENTAL HEALTH JOURNEY

LAUREN GREEN

Ballast Books, LLC
www.ballastbooks.com

ISBN: 978-1-966786-26-9

Printed in the United States of America

Cover Design by Savannah Spidalieri
Layout by Suzanne Uchytil

Published by Ballast Books
www.ballastbooks.com

For more information, bulk orders, appearances, or speaking requests,
please email: info@ballastbooks.com

For Jordan

AUTHOR'S NOTE

I was twelve years old when I realized I had a story to tell. Not a mystery or a drama like I normally wrote. A real story. One that might matter to someone. One that could change me—and with a bit of luck, maybe even the rest of the world. (Corny, I know—but hey, I'm an optimist.)

A year or so before, my little sister had been diagnosed with a mental illness. At the time, I had no idea what a mental illness was, but I figured it out pretty quickly as I watched Katie repeatedly harm herself and attempt to take her own life. Something unrecognizable emerged inside of her and swallowed her whole.

It was terrifying. I felt hopeless, helpless, useless. I was no match against the shadow that stirred behind my sister's eyes and changed her into a different person. I didn't have control over anything . . . at least I felt like I didn't.

It was my mom who inspired me. Understandably daunted by the prospect of raising a kid with mental health challenges, my mom went straight to the bookstore when Katie was diagnosed. She had no idea what she was doing or what she was up against, so she sought as much information as she could find to arm herself with background knowledge. Unfortunately, she discovered only a few books regarding childhood mental illness. And the books she did find offered only a clinical form of help, simply stating definitions, symptoms, and treatment options. There was no human advice, no encouragement. She felt like she and my dad were the only parents in the world who were trying to raise a child living with mental illness. It was a very lonely feeling.

It made my young heart ache to see my parents so lost, scared, and alone. I knew there wasn't much that I could do to help them, but I figured I could help future families dealing with the same thing. So, I decided to gain control over my family's circumstances in my own way by providing some piece of the information my parents so desperately searched for.

I was inexperienced as a writer, so I didn't make much meaningful progress at first. But that turned out to be a good thing for a couple of reasons.

First of all, the purpose behind my writing broadened as I grew older and became aware of the stigma associated with mental illness. I realized that I not only wanted to help families struggling with mental illness feel connected, but I also wanted to show that mental illness is nothing to be ashamed of and nothing to judge someone for.

I thought if people could see my sister as a person first, it would help chip away at the stigma. See, Katie lives with a mental illness that she never asked for and never wanted. But her mental health is only one aspect of her personhood. She's also a daughter, sister, friend, and loved one. She has a good heart and a bright mind. She can make a great difference in this world, just like anyone else—with or without a mental illness. Ultimately, mental illness doesn't define her or define anybody. It's a sickness, just like diabetes or cancer—not a choice. Stigma shouldn't even come into the picture.

Second of all, my family's story was still unfolding, making it difficult for me to plan the content of my book. I wrote down what I could over time, but it was difficult to conquer such an enormous and emotionally draining task without a clear plan in mind.

Eventually though, I realized my family's story would always be developing, no matter how much time passed. Katie has a mental illness. It's a permanent part of who she is (at least until we discover some sort of cure). And if her story does stop, that means she's not here anymore to continue it, and that's the last thing I want. So, with ample help and support from my parents and sisters, I was finally able to get our journey on paper.

This story is mine and my family's and everyone's. It's yours too. It's meant to offer advice, bring solace, crush the stigma, and start a conversation. It's meant to give hope. Whether you're dealing with mental illness yourself, living with someone who has a mental illness, or simply interested in the subject, I hope you get everything you need out of our story. And remember: whatever you're going through, you're not alone.

PROLOGUE

She fluttered and flapped, brilliant with color and life. She wanted to see, to learn, to experience, to thrive. Fear and pain and suffering simply didn't exist. Her world was her own.

As she soared through the air, dizzy with hope and happiness, she knew nothing but comfort and familiarity. If shadows skulked in her head—teasing, taunting, waiting—she ignored them. Nothing could touch her.

It was as if she didn't even realize how delicate she was. How fragile.

At some point, her mind began to twist, plaguing her with dejection and self-doubt. Her head, once filled with extravagant ideas and blind joy, was suddenly brimming over with blood and death and hatred. The lurking shadows chortled, charmed by her inescapable anguish.

As she plummeted into despondence, she noticed her wings beating gently into glass. Nudging her back. Keeping her in place. It seemed she was trapped inside an invisible prison.

She became claustrophobic and flew around frantically, desperate to escape, but the glass was a seamless cage. She was hopelessly confined, stuck in her own head, fixated on her ubiquitous thoughts of anxiety and despair.

What butterfly could survive in a bell jar?

Don't be afraid of
your story. It will
inspire others.

—*Unknown*

PART 1

LAUREN

Fall 1999

M y sister and I argued furiously as we strode toward Mommy's car, both of us shivering in the chilly breeze of an in-between season. We were probably disagreeing over what game we'd play when we got home or what music we'd listen to in the car. We always found a reason to fight.

Night had just fallen, and the sky was a dusky purple-blue, draping Nana and Papa's backyard in darkness. It must have rained that day; we could hear the water rushing past in the creek behind the swing set. Fireflies glowed in and out of existence around us, and crickets we could never find sang shrilly, just out of sight.

Our sweet, angry, little girl voices interrupted the peaceful scene of evening as we marched toward the car, but we were careful not to argue too loudly lest Mommy and Daddy hear—then we'd both be in trouble.

Since I was older by two and a half years, I walked half a step ahead of Katie, leading the way. She was being awfully mean to me, making fun of me or something, but I still let her sit behind the driver's seat so she would be closer to Mommy, who always drove unless she'd had too many glasses of wine.

As usual, I was calm and reserved, patiently waiting for Mommy and Daddy to come out, while Katie was wild and giddy, bouncing around in her seat. Pretty soon, I was irritated with her never-ending energy, and she was thinking it was real funny to poke me repeatedly.

I did not think it was real funny at all. In fact, I thought it was real obnoxious.

After about the fifth time asking her to *please* cut it out, I lost my temper. Lips pursed together in anger, I grabbed both of her hands and smashed them together, pushing them far away from me. When she squiggled and squirmed, I squeezed her wrists angrily, commanding her to quit it.

Eventually, Katie fell silent and still. Believing she'd finally relented, I released her wrists and breathed a soundless sigh of relief. Who ever thought a three-year-old could be so aggravating?

It happened quickly. Katie, enraged, grabbed my hand and sank her sharp teeth deep into my wrist. She usually looked like an angel with her white-blond ringlets and deep blue eyes, but in that moment, her hard face and hellhound teeth told a different story.

With slitted eyes, Katie released my wrist, leaving an outline of each of her little teeth in my flesh. Stunned, I cradled my arm gently in my lap and gulped back sobs.

Moments later, Katie and I both looked up as yellow light split the darkness and revealed Nana and Papa's cars in the garage. Mommy and Daddy were walking through the back door and hugging and kissing Nana and Papa goodbye.

I glanced at Katie, whose eyes had filled with terror. She shouldn't have been surprised; after all, the whole point of us waiting in the car was to encourage Mommy and Daddy to hurry up because we were ready to go home. However, she seemed to have forgotten about that and was now dreading the trouble she'd be in if Mommy and Daddy saw the angry red marks on my wrist.

Whereas I was sweet to the point of having no personality, Katie was an unremitting troublemaker. She often sidestepped serious discipline by cracking jokes and making Mommy and Daddy laugh, but she still got in trouble more than anyone else I knew.

Katie didn't seem like she was ready to resign herself to yet another punishment without trying some kind of defense. She stared unseeingly at me, clearly thinking rapidly. I watched her, tears still coursing quietly down my sodden cheeks, ready to tell on her as soon as our parents got in the car.

Suddenly, a quick, sly smile flashed across her face. I didn't know what her plan was, but her smug look told me it was a good one.

Mommy and Daddy were halfway to the car when she did it. I looked on in incredulous horror as Katie brought her own arm to her mouth and bit down as hard as she could. Tears immediately filled her eyes. Then, with a devilish smile in my direction, she started wailing.

I instantly knew what she was trying to do. I had only a moment to ponder just how far Katie would go to evade reprimand and get back at me. It seemed unthinkable that a little girl would do something like that. Was this typical sibling rivalry? Or was this a sign that something dark lurked somewhere inside Katie?

Little did I know that a few years later, around the time she was diagnosed, the image of Katie biting herself would become common. However, at that moment, all I could focus on was the world of hurt I was sure to be in if her wild plan worked.

Mommy and Daddy instantly ran over and yanked open Katie's door—the one that was facing the garage. For a moment, they simply took in the vision of both of us crying and cradling our arms. Mommy, who looked like a grown-up version of Katie, seemed very concerned as she asked what was wrong. Daddy, who looked more similar to me with dark hair and eyes, glared suspiciously at us, sure that we'd been up to no good (because, of course, we had been up to no good).

"What the hell happened?" he barked.

"L-Lauren b-b-bit me, and then she bit herself so she wouldn't get in trouble!" sobbed Katie in her sweetest, most innocent voice. I had to give her credit—she was exceptionally convincing. I hated her for it.

I opened my mouth indignantly to tell the true story, but nobody would listen. I could only imagine how the scene looked to our parents: one child bawling loudly and commandingly and the other crying earnestly but quietly, unwilling to show weakness. One look at my parents' faces, and I knew that they believed Katie and would never believe me.

Daddy drew himself up to his full height, and the anger on his face was awful to behold. We both shrank back automatically, terrified of him.

And then he exploded, shouting in The Voice, our name for the gruff, threatening tone he used when he was furious beyond imagining, and close—if not committed—to smacking our bottoms. He yelled about how often we fought, how we never listened, how we made it impossible to go out anywhere, how we embarrassed my parents every time. Then, he turned on me specifically and shouted himself hoarse.

I was so distraught, I barely listened. I supposed I could kind of understand why they misunderstood the situation, but I was hurt and outraged and disbelieving all the same. How could they take her seriously without even asking for my side of the story?

Finally, Daddy seemed to have exhausted his anger. He and Mommy settled themselves into the car, and we backed out of the driveway, the car's headlights illuminating the front hedges, then the mailbox, then the paved road as Mommy turned the steering wheel and shifted gears.

For a moment, I thought dully about the sheer unfairness of the situation, dreading arriving at home when I'd surely have to deal with the consequences of "my actions." Then, exhausted by reality, I closed my eyes on the scenery flashing past in the window.

I pretended to be asleep the whole way home.

LAUREN

Summer 2000

I t was Katie's birthday. I *hated* Katie's birthday. She always acted like an even bigger brat than usual, thinking she could get away with anything on her special day. She was wrong. My parents cut her a lot of slack, but she always pushed too hard and ended up getting into trouble.

I stared stonily at her stupid blonde pigtails as we sat in the grass around my Aunt Molly and Uncle Jim's patio. (The children weren't allowed to sit in seats; those were for adults only.)

Katie was wearing her brand-new birthday outfit—a white flowered dress with pink sleeves. She looked cute as a button. Ugh.

"I can't believe I'm four." Katie grinned. She looked so smug.

"I'm six. You'll never be older than me."

"But it's my birthday, not yours."

I wanted to smack her.

"Who's ready for presents?" sang Mommy as she walked outside with a bunch of colorfully wrapped gifts in her arms.

"Me! Me me me!" shouted Katie, who'd been asking Mommy when she could open her presents every twenty minutes since we'd arrived.

"You can sit in my seat while I take pictures." Mommy smiled indulgently.

I moped around the yard while Katie was opening her gifts. I always became a little jealous when she got a bunch of new things and I didn't, especially when she gloated about it.

The next present to open was Aunt Molly and Uncle Jim's. As a joke, they had gotten her some fake poop since every time they'd asked her what she wanted for her birthday, she'd answered "poop" before laughing uproariously. They waited with bated breath as she ripped open the wrapping paper and removed the lid from the newly revealed box.

There was a brief moment of silence. Then, quite abruptly, Katie's whole face turned bright red, and she hurled the poop across the patio. "I don't want the poop!" she screamed, absolutely furious.

Her fury was so hot, so explosive, so irrational. In moments like this, she became so much angrier than anyone else would be in the same situation. Looking back on it now, it seems possible that such an extreme response to such a silly scenario might have been a sign that something was different about Katie. However, at the time, the sight of a cherub-cheeked four-year-old getting mad over some fake poop was simply comical. Everyone roared with laughter, hardly able to breathe in response to the hilarity of the scene. Mom, Aunt Molly, and Aunt Maggie all had tears dripping down their cheeks from laughing so hard.

"Katie, it was a joke. We thought you would like it," choked Aunt Molly, holding her stomach, tears still in her eyes. "Here's our real present." She pointed to another wrapped box, but Katie resolutely turned away.

"No. I want Grandma and Grandpa's present next." Cries of laughter followed this pronouncement as well. Katie simmered with anger through the rest of her presents.

I didn't really understand what was so funny at the time, especially since I was so busy feeling bad for myself over the fact that Katie was having a special day and I wasn't. But I didn't really gain any satisfaction from Katie's distress. Mostly, I was just confused. Katie was the kind of person who would *love* to receive poop as a present. In fact, in the following months, Katie would frequently play with her birthday poop. (Usually, she tried to prank me with it. Funny, funny girl.) But at the time, for whatever reason, Katie had absolutely no positive feelings about her bathroom-themed gift.

About an hour later, Katie seemed to have calmed down. She was playing with her new toys, rudely flaunting them to make me feel excluded.

"Come on, girls! It's time for dinner," announced Mommy, leading us to the dining room.

"Here, Katie. The birthday girl sits here," said Aunt Maggie, unable to suppress a mischievous grin.

Katie looked down at her plate. Someone had placed the fake poop on it.

"I said I don't *want* the poop!" she shrieked, flaring up once again as she flung the poop to the floor.

Everyone erupted in laughter, and Katie's cheeks and ears burned red.

LAUREN

Winter 2001

Sleep. Sleep sleep sleep.

I chanted the words over and over again in my head, futilely attempting to block out all other sound. Groaning, I flipped over on my back and pushed the ends of my pillow against my ears, turning my face from side to side restlessly.

I'd tried counting sheep. I'd tried emptying my mind. I'd tried thinking happy thoughts. I'd tried counting to a thousand. (Okay, maybe I'd skipped a few hundred digits, but it hadn't been working anyway.) Nothing would drown out the noises that had been drifting up from the bunk below for the past twenty minutes.

"Lauren. Lauren. Hey, Laaaauren. Are you listening to me? Huh?"

"Shutupshutupshutup," I groaned under my breath.

"Whaaaat?" Katie asked in a sing-song voice. Even though I couldn't see her, I knew the corners of her mouth were twisting up into her devilish smile.

"Shut up!" I snapped. "Go. To. Sleep."

"No."

"Katie, *please.*"

She simply cackled gleefully in response.

"Be *quiet.*"

"I don't want to. I don't wanna go to sleep."

"But I *do!*" I was almost crying with frustration. Huffing irritably, I secured the pillow more tightly around my ears and squeezed my eyes shut.

For a few seconds, there was a beautiful, blessed silence, interrupted only by Katie tossing and turning under her sheets. I sighed silently in relief, welcoming the quiet gratefully.

I should have known it wouldn't last long.

I sobbed audibly at the sound of her. Of all the things she could do to drive me crazy . . . The child was singing. *Singing.*

God help me.

"I like big butts, and I cannot lie—"

"Shut up!" I hissed.

She laughed.

Furious, I threw the pillow against the wall, pushed back my sheets, and clambered down the ladder of the bunk bed. Then, with my nose in the air and my hands on my hips, I marched angrily into the family room, where my dad and my very pregnant mom were watching TV.

"Mommy, Katie won't leave me alone."

Mom glanced exhaustedly at Dad, silently asking him not to yell. She'd grown tired of our nightly bedtime bickering and my dad's explosive reaction. It was clear that she wanted to avoid a showdown if possible. "Ignore her, Lauren."

"But—"

"Just try it, Lauren!"

Scowling, I shuffled back to my room and got back into bed.

"Did you like my singing?" Katie asked innocently.

I gritted my teeth and remained silent.

"Lauren?"

I bit my tongue to keep from answering. It was *so hard* not to snap back like usual.

"Lauren, are you asleep? Lauren? Lauren, Lauren, Lauren, Lauren?"

Finally, she stood up on her bed and peered through the wooden slats designed to prevent me from falling to the floor in my sleep.

"Lauren?"

I stared beadily at her. Her mouth dropped open, and she gazed at me incredulously as if she couldn't believe I was pointedly ignoring her.

"I'm telling," she chirped in an annoyingly superior voice. Without a moment's hesitation, she bounded off the bed and out the door.

"Mom, Lauren's ignoring me," I heard her say in indignation.

I smiled grimly as I heard my dad explode at her. When he finally placed her back in bed with one last admonishment, I let my eyes drift shut. *Finally.* I reveled in the silence, sinking into the mattress, waves of sleep lapping at the corners of my mind, pulling me under . . .

"Lauren?"

"Noo," I groaned, lightly hitting my forehead against the wall. *Here we go again.*

DAD

While there are countless theories about the proper way to deal with children, I've always believed that the key is firm limits and consistent follow-through. I have tried to apply this approach in raising all my children.

I'm one of those old-fashioned people who still believes in corporal punishment. I see absolutely nothing wrong in swatting a young child's behind when necessary. Accordingly, I would, when the situation warranted it, take my open hand to my children's rear ends.

I clearly recall one incident when Lauren and Katie were sharing a room with bunk beds. Katie was always difficult at bedtime, and on this particular occasion, I had already visited their room a couple of times to tell them to be quiet and go to sleep. So, when I went in there for the third time, I told them, "If I have to come back in here again, you will both get a spanking." Then, I returned to the family room where I soon heard more nonsense from their room. It was quieter than before, with Katie doing most of the talking and Lauren pleading with her to be quiet, as she didn't want to get spanked.

My great-grandmother was fond of saying that to be a good parent, you sometimes need to "be a little bit deaf and a little bit blind." I was following her advice and overlooking their whispers until my wife, Anne, came by and yelled at them for talking and not going to sleep. With Anne's scolding, I could no longer ignore the behavior and was forced to follow through with the spanking I had promised.

I went in and gave them both a couple of light swats on their behinds. Although I had intentionally been very gentle, Lauren reacted by crying, as she never wanted to disappoint. Katie's response, on the other hand, was "Hah! It didn't even hurt!" I ignored her comment, and they soon fell asleep.

A week or so later, Katie got into trouble again, and I made sure she wouldn't say it didn't hurt this time around. As I walked away, I could hear Katie say through her sobbing, "It hurt this time . . . Why did it have to hurt?"

"Perhaps you shouldn't have bragged that it didn't hurt last time," replied Anne.

While I believe spanking has its place, I only resorted to it when everything else failed. Generally, I would just take things away and use what the girls referred to as "The Voice." The girls would usually respond fairly quickly when I used The Voice, so I seldom had to resort to anything else. Nonetheless, there were plenty of times when Katie pushed me and pushed me until I smacked her bottom—almost as if she wanted to test me to see how far she could go.

LAUREN

Spring 2001

Daddy burst into our room in the middle of the night, yanking us from our sleep.

"Wake up! Wake up! Come on, get a move on! Your mother's having the baby!"

I scrambled clumsily down the bunk bed's ladder, still hazy from sleep. Katie hadn't gotten out of bed; she didn't seem to be quite awake yet.

"Let's go!" shouted Daddy, pulling her up unceremoniously. "Just put your shoes and coats on and get in the car."

We stumbled down the hall one after the other, trying to walk and put our shoes on at the same time. Somehow, we made it to the car where Mommy sat in the passenger seat, breathing deeply but calmly. Ten minutes later, we were at Grandma and Grandpa's house. There were lights shining in the downstairs windows, faintly illuminating the quiet front porch.

Within moments, we were inside, and Mommy and Daddy were backing swiftly out of the driveway. We waved goodbye to them with Grandma and Grandpa until they were out of sight.

"All right, girls! Bedtime." My grandma was wearing her nightgown and slippers, and she looked as lovely and sweet as she had a few hours earlier, when we'd been at dinner celebrating her seventieth birthday.

Grandma led us up the stairs and into the end bedroom that my mom and aunt used to share. There were two twin beds with matching floral comforters beckoning us to sleep. I took the one closest to the window, and Katie took the one closest to the door. Grandma kissed us both good night and tiptoed out, making sure the nightlight near the door was on.

I was nearing the cusp of oblivion when Katie's voice pulled me from the brink.

"Lauren, I have a bloody nose." Her voice was muffled because she had her hands cupped over the lower half of her face.

"Oh no," I groaned, bleary from exhaustion. "I'll get tissues." Trying to be quiet and quick, I raced to the bathroom down the hall, where I snatched a handful of tissues before shooting back to the bedroom. "Here," I said breathlessly, tossing the tissues on the bed in front of her. "Did you get blood all over the place?"

"No." Her voice was thick as she pressed the entire bundle of tissues against her face. "I need more."

Scowling, I made another trip to the bathroom, bringing a huge wad of toilet paper this time. "Have you been picking your nose again?" I demanded as I shoved the toilet paper at her.

"No!"

"Yeah, right."

After a couple more trips to the bathroom, it seemed Katie's bloody nose was under control. But Grandma must have heard my little feet pattering back and forth across the hallway. Looking wan and worried, she appeared in the doorway just as I was climbing back into bed.

"Are you girls all right?"

"Yeah, Katie just got a bloody nose."

"Oh my goodness! What can I do?"

"It's okay. I think it's almost over now," responded Katie through the toilet paper she still had clamped to her nose.

"Okay, well . . . Try to go back to sleep, all right? And wake me up if anything else happens."

"Okay."

"Grandma, is it your birthday yet?" asked Katie.

"Yes, it is." Grandma smiled. "And you know what? I think it's going to be your little sister's birthday too."

Sarah was born a little later that morning. After a short night's rest, Grandma and Grandpa shepherded us to the car, and we drove up to the hospital to visit Mommy, Daddy, and our new baby sister. I was still wearing my long pink nightshirt featuring Meg from *Hercules* because we hadn't brought a change of clothes.

"Wow," I murmured, looking at what appeared to be a pink, pinched alien.

"Huh," said Katie.

We both stared at her, unimpressed. We had no idea then, but little Sarah was changing our family in a beautiful and meaningful way. She would drive us nuts in the years to come, but she would become a strong and vibrant part of our sisterhood—and of my family's story.

LAUREN

Fall 2001

It was the perfect day for a wedding. The sky was blue with a few cotton swab clouds hanging about. Though it was October, the weather was ideal—not too hot or too cold. And the little church looked so pretty, the emerald grass surrounding it sparkling with dew that hadn't quite evaporated yet.

"You girls ready?" asked Mommy, looking even more beautiful than usual in her wedding outfit and makeup.

"Yes!"

Katie and I looked almost identical with matching hair, shoes, and dresses. The only difference was the velvet top of my dress was maroon while Katie's was forest green.

"Where's Sarah?" asked Katie.

"She's with the babysitter. Now, remember: Caroline is going to be in the back of the church with Sarah for the whole ceremony. Once you're done with your part, go on back and join them, okay?"

"Okay," we said in unison.

"Great. The wedding's starting soon, so let's go inside and get into our spots."

We traipsed back into the church and waited in the dressing room. It was kind of small, and we had already spent a lot of time in there when getting ready, so we bounced around, anxious to get going.

"Do you remember the plan?" I asked Katie.

"Yes."

"Okay, good."

"You're so bossy."

"Girls! It's almost your turn!" my aunt called quietly from just outside.

We turned and grinned at each other before scrambling out into the hall, our Mary Jane heels clacking crazily on the linoleum floor.

"Shh! Here are your flower girl wreaths." They seemed to be made of twigs with flowers clustered at the bottom and a bow tying it all together. "Okay, go!" She pushed lightly on our backs, and we lurched forward, a little bit cowed by all the eyes suddenly fixed on us.

I pasted a smile on my face and glanced sideways at Katie, whose mouth was agape. "Smile!" I hissed between my teeth, and she instantly started beaming.

As planned, Katie and I snuck to the back of the church after fulfilling our flower girl duties. Sarah was pretty fussy, so we just helped Caroline keep her calm and quiet until it was time for the reception.

Since we were technically part of the wedding party, we had to wait until the DJ announced us to enter the dimly lit reception hall. When we skipped inside together, holding hands, everyone started cooing over how cute we were, and we laughed, in love with all the attention we were getting.

Katie and I were pretty bored during dinner and the speeches, especially since we were the only kids there. So, once everyone had finished eating and the bride and groom had had their first dance, we made our way to the dance floor, itching to actually *do* something.

I feel good! I knew that I would . . .

"I love this song!" screeched Katie, jumping with glee. "Let's dance!"

Grabbing each other's hands, we started spinning around and around, enjoying the feel of our dresses swishing around our calves.

"Aw, you two are so cute! Let me get a picture."

We posed for the stranger, our arms around each other, our cheeks pressed together. Then, reveling in the attention we were drawing, we continued to dance around all night, giggling and hugging nonstop.

"It's so nice to see you two getting along," said my mom with a smile.

Katie, who had always been a little bit taller and stronger than me, picked me right up and tried to swing me around. We both lost balance and crashed to the floor. Mommy rushed forward, clearly afraid this would be the end of our moment of peace. But before she could get there, Katie had hopped to her feet and was reaching down to help me up.

"Thanks," I giggled. Then, we went on dancing, though everyone had grown tired of our exuberant moves and no longer twittered over how endearing we were.

Katie and I fought a lot—that's for sure. But as many bad moments as we had, we also had countless good ones. And that's still true today, now that we're adults. No matter what, despite each of our faults, we love each other unconditionally.

This Katie—the Katie who lived with abandon, the Katie who danced and laughed and helped her sister up when she fell down—is my sister. Regardless of how her mental illness affects her, she will always be this Katie. She will always be beautiful and strong and loving. Because Katie's mental illness doesn't define her. It's just one small part of an amazing girl who will do amazing things. Just you wait and see.

LAUREN

Spring 2002

"You're a buttface."

"You're mean."

"Buttface."

"Well, you have a fat head!" I exploded.

"Now, Lauren," said Katie in her loftiest tone. "We don't say 'fat head.' We say I have a very *large* head."

"Girls," admonished Grandma from the driver's seat of the car, but she was laughing. "Settle down back there."

Moments later, she parked in front of the Sears at the mall and helped us out of our car seats.

"What are we having for lunch, Grandma?" asked Katie excitedly.

"Grandma already said we're getting Pasta House!" I said bossily. We always went there for lunch when we spent the day with Grandma. It was a little Italian restaurant nestled in one of the corners of the mall, and it sort of felt like a tradition to eat there on our days off from elementary school.

"That's right. We're going to Pasta House," said Grandma placatingly, trying to avert an argument.

Katie stuck her tongue out at me when Grandma wasn't looking.

"All right," sighed Grandma when we were seated at a table near the back. "Pasta con broccoli for lunch?"

"Yes!" we chorused, in agreement for perhaps the first time all day.

"Oh, look. They have chocolate," exclaimed Katie, pointing at the bowl in the middle of the table. It was filled with slabs of butter wrapped in gold foil.

"Oh, yeah. Chocolate," I scoffed.

Katie grabbed one eagerly and looked at it for several seconds. Then, she started to unwrap it. "Ooh, *white* chocolate!" she said enthusiastically.

It seemed impossible that she hadn't noticed BUTTER in large letters across the label, and I was kind of interested to see what would happen next, so I didn't say anything. The next second, she pushed the butter out of the foil and right into her mouth.

"Puhh," she gagged, spitting the butter back into the foil.

"Katie! What are you doing!" gasped Grandma, who had been looking at the menu, not paying attention to our conversation. "That was very rude."

"Lauren let me eat butter!" cried Katie, her face glowing angrily. "It's her fault!"

"No, it's not! You're the dummy who ate butter!"

"Girls! That's enough. If you don't stop fighting, we won't go to the toy store after lunch."

That was enough to convince us to shape up. So, after lunch, we rode the escalator up to the second floor, where KB Toys was located.

Every time Grandma took us to the toy store, Katie and I each picked out a Polly Pocket. But every time Grandma took us to the toy store, we still made several circuits around the place, determined to get something *other* than Polly Pockets.

"What about these, Lauren?"

"ClipHits? I dunno. Those were kind of dumb last time we got them."

"Yeah," Katie agreed, instantly shoving them back onto the shelf. "They were kinda dumb."

She stayed close behind me the whole time we were in the store and earnestly asked my opinion on every mildly interesting toy we passed.

Looking back now, it's clear to see that Katie looked up to me. Even though we bickered incessantly, I can tell now that she wanted my love and approval. Blinded by our volatile relationship, I just thought she was annoying. But now, having a better understanding of Katie and her core beliefs, I realize that she wanted to be like me, even though we're very different people with distinct personalities and talents.

This would become a problem when Katie's mental illness started to take over. She would constantly compare herself to me and inexplicably conclude that she was stupid or difficult or inferior. It's hard to understand why she would feel that way, since she's such an intelligent, compassionate, personable individual. I suppose, for some reason, she put too much stock in the skills that I possess and not enough stock in the many skills she possesses. Regardless, this dynamic between us, which was evident so many years before Katie's diagnosis, was a dangerous one.

Forty-five minutes later, we skipped out of the store, smiling broadly, thanking Grandma profusely. We each had a new Polly Pocket in our hands.

MOM

Summer 2002

Katie and Lauren were fighting all the time—to the point that we were getting complaints from daycare and babysitters. In fact, some babysitters wouldn't even come back because they fought so frequently. Eventually, Rob and I just didn't even know what to do. Timeouts didn't work. Yelling didn't work. Spanking didn't work. The fighting went on and on!

One day, Rob ended up taking both girls back to our bedroom and having a serious talk with them.

"Okay, this is what's gonna happen," he said in a low, menacing voice. "You guys are going to start getting along. You are not going to be fighting all the time. We are not going to be getting calls from daycare. And if it continues, I am going to use my belt."

Lauren became very distraught and understood immediately, *Oh, Dad's serious, and I don't want that to happen.* But Katie looked at him and smiled. So, Rob felt that he needed to get through to Katie that he wasn't joking around—that he was really going to do what he said. He took his belt off and whipped it across a wooden chest that was at the base of our bed, and it smacked really hard. That got Katie's attention.

It also got my attention.

I was in the family room, sitting on the sofa just bawling my eyes out because I was not actually going to allow that kind of punishment to ever happen. My siblings had been severely beaten as discipline when I was growing up, and I had no intention of allowing my kids to feel as scared and helpless as I'd felt as a child. So, later, Rob and I had a frank discussion about everything.

"Okay," I began. "So, I know that when you put a threat out there, you're going to follow through with it. But just so that you know, you're not following through with that one. You will never do that. That's not going to happen."

Of course, Rob didn't *want* to do it. And luckily, things actually ended up improving, so this never became an issue. But that just goes to show how often Lauren and Katie would quarrel—constantly!

LAUREN

Fall 2002

When Katie was in first grade and I was in third, we became close friends with a fifth grader named Heather who lived down the street from us. Katie and I came to look up to Heather because she seemed to know so much about the world. Our mother essentially invited her into our family because she was worried that Heather's home life wasn't that great; her mother didn't seem to be concerned about her whereabouts most of the time. As a result, we spent quite a lot of time together.

We spent all of that fall going "acorn hunting" around our neighborhood, which was safe enough that we were allowed a limited amount of freedom to explore as long as we were home well before dark and told Mom where we were going.

Katie, Heather, and I took our plastic green and yellow wagon up the street and around the cul-de-sac, stopping at each yard to gather all the acorns strewn across the thirsty grass. We filled up several blue buckets, pretending that we were collecting food for the winter. Mommy would be horrified weeks later when we got bored of the game and dumped hundreds of acorns all over our own backyard.

One time, when we were halfway down the cul-de-sac that looped behind our house, a beat-up green sedan came down the road and slowed down until it was moving at the same pace as we were walking. A large woman with long, dark hair and sunglasses sat behind the wheel, perhaps watching us. I didn't think much of it, busy as I was with picking out acorns, but Katie became very agitated.

"Lauren, that lady is following us!" she whispered, leaning in my direction, eyes darting around.

"She's probably just looking for an address or something."

"No, she's looking right at me."

"How do you know? She's wearing sunglasses."

"She talked to me, Lauren! She wants to kidnap us!" Katie hissed loudly, her face turning red.

"Ooh, I bet she does!" Heather chimed in with relish. She tended to be pretty dramatic and loved running away with her imagination. It was fun most of the time, but sometimes she cultivated unnecessary fear and anxiety in us. Considering our mother also spent a lot of time ensuring we were intensely wary of our surroundings, it seemed we were doomed to a life of paranoia.

Maybe Katie's concern was bred purely from Mom's constant reminders to kick and scream and run away if someone tried to grab us. Having regular conversations about that sort of thing put both of us on edge. But it's also possible that her paranoia represented the beginnings of mental illness. Either way, when Heather indicated she agreed the woman was suspicious, it seemed to confirm all Katie's fears—and trigger mine.

"What?" I dropped an acorn, suddenly feeling nervous.

"Lauren, I'm scared." Katie's face was white now. My nervousness increased, and suddenly, I was just as convinced as they were that we were about to be kidnapped.

"Let's go home, okay?" I said in a would-be casual voice.

I put the bucket in the back of the wagon and let Katie and Heather hop in as I yanked at the handle and dragged them along. The girls murmured back and forth behind me as I shuffled briskly home, trying not to notice the green car, which eventually went around the cul-de-sac but caught up with us again as we were approaching our house.

"Come on!" I whispered loudly, dropping the handle of the wagon in front of our next-door neighbor's yard and running up our driveway, Katie and Heather close behind me.

That wasn't the only time Katie's paranoia came through. A few months later, Mommy sent Katie and I to walk Heather home since it was dark outside, and she didn't want her to walk alone.

About halfway down the hill, a red truck slowed down next to us. Heather and I weren't particularly concerned at first, but Katie was instantly alarmed, and her distress incited fear in us too.

For a few moments, we whispered to each other in a panic, trying to figure out what to do. I insisted that he was probably lost, but Katie was convinced he was about to grab all three of us.

When the man parked in the desolate gravel drive next to Heather's house, all three of us lost it. Without even conferring with one another, we all shrieked, darted behind the nearest house, and ran through everyone's backyards until we were back home.

LAUREN

Summer 2003

"You guys ready?" asked Caroline.

"Yes!" Katie and I chorused, both grinning from ear to ear.

It was summer. That meant no school, longer days, and pool time galore. Basically, it was the best time of the year. Unfortunately, both of our parents worked, so we couldn't spend time with them. And Sarah went to daycare every day as usual. On the bright side, Caroline, a high-schooler who lived down the street, was babysitting us for the summer. She was really pretty and nice. Most importantly, she had a car to drive us around in!

"Are we picking up Anna too?"

"Ye-*es*!" screeched Katie as she bounded out the front door, towel flying behind her.

Anna and Katie had become best friends from the moment they'd met at Meet and Greet, otherwise known as kindergarten orientation. Two years later, they were still inseparable. Unless one of my friends was available, I was typically resigned to the role of third wheel.

We scrambled into the back seat of Caroline's silver sedan and buckled our seat belts, Katie with much grumbling. We were both wearing colorful swimsuits, flip flops, and ponytails. Our pink and orange beach towels lay bunched up between us in the middle seat. We jittered with excitement.

As soon as Caroline started the ignition, her "Oldies but Goodies" CD began playing. Content, I sang along to "Build Me Up, Buttercup," one of my favorite songs, but Katie huffed loudly.

"Can we listen to this?" she asked in a loud, demanding voice. Trying not to take her eyes off the road, Caroline reached her hand back to take the CD Katie was thrusting at her: the *Shrek* soundtrack.

"Ooh, can we listen to track three?" I asked, deciding not to question why Katie had *my* CD in her possession.

"Yep!"

I sang along to this song too, gazing out the window at the houses and trees. Katie sang as well. However, as opposed to my soft, innocuous voice pointed out the window, Katie's voice rang loud and clear throughout the car. She sure loved to make a racket.

As soon as my song ended, I felt Katie suddenly get very still, then quiver with anticipation. I looked around curiously at her, then rolled my eyes when I realized that she was just excited for the next song to come on.

Considering Katie was seven and I was nine, we were obviously strictly forbidden from cursing of any kind. Even fairly mild forms of cursing were liable to earn us a timeout. But Katie loved bending the rules. She found every possible way to push as far as she could without getting in trouble. And when it came to cursing, music was Katie's way of bending the rules.

"I DON'T GIVE A DAMN 'BOUT MY REPUTATION," she bellowed.

If she had been singing loudly before, it was nothing compared to her volume now. I glared at her and pursed my lips, discreetly warning her that she was begging to get in trouble. She grinned cheekily at me and kept right on singing, emphasizing the word "damn" every time it came up in the song.

Caroline glanced at Katie in the rearview mirror but refrained from speaking. She had obviously learned that it was best to pick your battles when it came to Katie's wild antics. I had yet to learn that trick. Being the goody-two-shoes perfectionist that I was, I couldn't bear for Katie to get away with blatantly flouting the rules.

"Caroline, Katie's saying a bad word," I pointed out in my most dignified voice as we approached Anna's house.

"No, I'm just singing the song!" Katie interjected quickly before Caroline could respond.

I opened my mouth to retort, but Caroline cut me off as she parked in the driveway. "Go up to the door and get Anna, okay, Katie?"

Katie sent me a wicked little smile and jumped out of the car, leaving the door wide as she ran to ring the doorbell. Moments later, Anna was sliding into the middle seat next to me, knocking our towels to the floor. As we pulled out of the driveway and the two best friends chattered and squirmed next to me, I realized that a new song was playing, even though Katie's song had only just begun when we arrived at Anna's house.

Our neighborhood pool was only five minutes away, but Anna and Katie had way too much energy to stand being cooped up in a car for any amount of time. The very moment Caroline pulled into a parking spot, the two girls shot out of the car and sprinted through the gates to the check-in desk.

"Walk!" shouted Caroline, but they were already gone.

I grabbed the towels and goggles they'd left behind and trailed behind Caroline to the desk. Anna and Katie were just finishing up signing us all in. As soon as that was in order, we walked as quickly as we could (no running allowed) to the chairs by the deep end.

While Caroline laid her towel out and settled onto it to tan, we kids shuffled over to the pool. Katie and Anna preferred to cannonball right into the water. I liked to ease my way in. As I slowly stepped down the rungs of the ladder leading into the deeper end of the pool, Katie landed in the water right next to me, intentionally drenching me.

"Hey!" I shrieked, shivering with cold. "You suck." Taking a deep breath, I gave up on my usual tactic and swiftly slid the rest of the way into the water. Then, for good measure, I splashed Katie when she was least expecting it. To my chagrin, the tiny tide of water hitting her neck and cheek didn't seem to faze her at all.

We had several games we liked to play at the pool: Silence, Categories, Sharks and Minnows, Stars. That day, we decided to play Stars. To play, one person was selected to be "it," and they had the honor of choosing whatever movie they pleased. Then, they gave the initials of the movie (for example, BIO for *Bring It On*). If no one could guess based on that, they would give clues, such as actors' or characters' names, plot points, and movie rating. Whoever was first to swim across the deep end, tag the person's hand, and correctly name the movie got to be "it" next.

After several rounds of this, it got harder for the person who was "it" to think of clever new movies. So, we started a new game. While Katie, who was "it," thought of a movie, Anna and I, at the opposite side of the deep end, competed to see who could hold their breath underwater the longest.

We slowly sank to the bottom as we let the air drift from our lungs and bubble to the surface of the pool. It was a close match, but I won by a good two seconds. I zoomed to the surface triumphantly, gasping for air once my head broke through the water.

"Okay, I'm ready!" sang Katie. "FN."

With hardly a moment's hesitation, Anna shot through the water toward Katie. I still had no idea what the answer was.

"Clue!" I shouted desperately, but Anna had already reached Katie and slapped her hand.

"Stars, *Finding Nemo*!" she shouted.

"Yep!" Katie swam back to me, a strange smile on her face. "Bet you can't beat me," she said when she arrived by my side, bobbing at the edge of the deep end.

"Betcha I can!" I countered before we both dove into the water.

Again, I managed to stay down for a couple of seconds longer. When I reached the top, I was feeling victorious. The truth was I hadn't expected to actually win against either of them. Now I had won against both of them!

"Are you ready, Anna?" I asked.

"Yeah! WWATCF!"

Katie twitched as if about to shoot off from the side of the pool but remained where she was.

"Clue!" I asked.

"It's about lots of candy."

Instantly, Katie was off. After a moment, I thought of something it could be. I half-heartedly raced after her, but she was way ahead of me.

"Stars, *Willy Wonka and the Chocolate Factory!*"

I paddled back to the other side of the deep end, scowling. Anna joined me with a grin on her face. "Ready to race?"

This went on a couple more times before I began to get aggravated and suspicious. Anna and Katie were somehow able to guess each other's answer immediately each time. Simultaneously, the amount of time they spent holding their breaths between rounds diminished.

It took me longer than it should have to realize they were cheating. I had always been taught that you should treat others as you'd like to be treated. With this in mind, I made the faulty assumption that if I treated people a certain way, they would treat me the same way back. Unfortunately, that is not the case.

When Anna was "it" and Katie was racing me, I got smart. She was barely at the bottom of the pool for two seconds before she flew to the top. Unbeknownst to her, I shot up right behind her. My ears caught the end of Anna telling Katie the movie she was going to choose.

"Are you serious? You've been cheating this whole time?" My voice rose as I became more and more upset. "I can't believe you. I never would have thought you'd do that. I'm never playing a game with you again!"

Katie merely laughed. There was a certain meanness about her that didn't necessarily fit with her personality. She didn't seem quite like herself. "You're so dumb. I can't believe it took you so long to figure it out."

I swelled with outrage at her mocking and blatant lack of apology. "Never playing a game with you *again*," I repeated tremulously, yanking myself out of the water and stomping to find my towel.

LAUREN

Fall 2004

"What are you doing?" I asked Katie, joining her on the bottom step of the staircase leading to the second floor.

"I'm in timeout." She scowled, her small, childish face contorted with petulance.

"What'd you do this time?" I sighed exaggeratedly.

"Nothing."

I scoffed. Katie spent probably a quarter of her time in timeout. Almost every single time we went to Grandma and Grandpa's for holidays or birthday celebrations, she found her way to the foot of the stairs, a frown darkening her face. Daddy would snap at her to stop being disrespectful. She would grin and continue doing whatever she was doing. Daddy would give her one more chance. Katie would push and push and push until, finally, Daddy would snap, yell, and send her to the bottom step. It was practically a tradition in our family.

"Grandpa yelled at me." Well, that was new. Grandpa was just as gruff as Daddy though, so I wasn't that surprised.

"Aw, I bet that was scary. He kinda scares me sometimes."

"Yeah, it was *so* scary."

We sat in companionable silence for a few moments. Then, I directed my gaze to the purple bin that Grandma kept all our toys in next to the front door.

"Wanna play the ball game?"

Katie and I had invented a game in which one of us stood at the foot of the stairs and the other sat at the top and we threw a soft green ball to each other. It wasn't particularly exciting, but it was something to do when we got bored. It was about the only thing we *could* do when Katie was in timeout.

"Sure." She smiled, her cheeks dimpling.

Katie was always a difficult child. She was stubborn, rowdy, and a little bit selfish. However, in spite of her more abrasive qualities, Katie always had a good heart and always loved fiercely. She was my most loyal friend.

Essentially, she was just like any sister, any daughter, any human being. She was normal. It was impossible for me to imagine at that point that one day, Katie would be rocking on the ground at my grandparents' house, lost in the throes of her mental illness. I had no idea that my funny, energetic, strong little sister would soon be transformed into something I could hardly recognize.

We giggled obliviously as we tossed the ball back and forth, perfectly content, entirely unprepared.

The only journey is
the journey within.

—*Rainer Maria Rilke*

PART 2

MOM

_____

Winter 2005

Katie was always a difficult child at home. She constantly tested the limits and knew what buttons to push. She would even
pick on Lauren, who was almost three years older. However, at
school, she was a perfect angel. At parent-teacher conferences,
the teachers would tell me how awesome Katie was. They would
say that she always followed directions and participated in classroom discussions. In response, I would always ask, "Are you *sure*
you've got the right person?"

That's why it was so strange to see such a dramatic shift in her
behavior at school.

It happened very suddenly when Katie was in third grade—just
eight years old. The kids had just gone back to school after Christmas
break. I began to notice papers that Katie had scrawled on, saying, "I
hate myself, I'm stupid, I'm fat, I wish I was dead." And she would
scribble really hard with pencil, making the paper shiny black.

At the same time, she began having meltdowns at home. "I hate myself," she'd say. "Everyone hates me. I wish I was dead."

After about a week of this behavior, I went up to school to talk to her teacher. Mrs. Karol was a heavyset middle-aged woman. I thought she seemed a little scary at first, but it turned out that she was about the most patient and understanding person ever!

When I asked her whether she had picked up on any changes in Katie, Mrs. Karol said that she'd definitely noticed a difference and was hoping it was just because Katie was getting back into the school routine after being off for a few weeks. She went on to tell me that Katie was being very disruptive in class, which was out of character for her. For instance, Katie had slammed a small ball down on the floor one day, and it had bounced and hit another child in the face. She was also getting up and moving around the class inappropriately. She would even sit underneath her desk and do other odd things like that. It wasn't like her at all.

I left the school that day very thankful for the honest feedback—and also crying my eyes out because something was clearly wrong with my daughter!

I vividly remember sitting in the parking lot at daycare, hardly aware of how I'd gotten there. I wanted to call our pediatrician before I went in to pick up Lauren, Katie, and Sarah. So, I called Dr. Lee, and she advised that we take her to see a psychiatrist. Thus began our first experience in the mental health arena.

Our pediatrician had given me a few names of psychiatrists she recommended. I then had to figure out who was accepting new patients and was covered by our health insurance plan. Unfortunately, this is not as easy as it may seem. None of the recommended psychiatrists were in my network. I thought Katie would be more comfortable with a female psychiatrist, so that narrowed my search. I called a couple of providers, but they weren't accepting new patients or couldn't get us in for months.

I was desperate. We needed help, and we needed it sooner rather than later!

Finally, I contacted Dr. Stanley, who would be able to see Katie as a therapist *and* as a psychiatrist, meaning she could prescribe medication while providing additional emotional support. She was recommended by Dr. Lee, so I felt comfortable with my decision.

When I called to schedule the appointment, she was accepting new patients and could see Katie in the next few weeks. However, she didn't accept any insurance or credit cards. Cash or check only, and payable prior to each visit! The cost was two hundred dollars per session. This wasn't ideal financially, but we were willing to do whatever it took to help Katie get better. And we just kind of learned as we went along to avoid psychiatrists with those kind of payment requirements.

Our first visit with Dr. Stanley was on February 15. This was more of a get-to-know-you session, and it was two hours long. Dr. Stanley met with me and Rob alone, then with Katie alone, and finally with all three of us together.

Part of the getting to know you included looking at family history. So, I started by sharing the story of my brother James's journey with mental illness.

James is nine years older than me, so I don't remember a lot about him growing up. I do remember that he was often in trouble. If I had been familiar with the symptoms at the time, I might have recognized that there was a larger problem at play.

When I was about nineteen and he was twenty-eight, James called my sister Maggie and told her that he had a gun and was going to kill himself. My sister and I lived together at the time, so she immediately told me what was going on. Of course, we both freaked out.

Our parents weren't in town because they had temporarily moved to Maryland for our dad's job. So, Maggie took responsibility for the situation. She grabbed her car keys and picked up James while I began reaching out to hospitals to see if they would take him if we brought him in.

I called hospital after hospital, explaining the situation, but each one told me that James would have to sign himself in or we would need to get a court order to have him admitted. Well, when you've got somebody who is suicidal, they're maybe not going to admit themselves. And it was a Saturday night, so a court order wasn't likely to happen. I became very frustrated and almost started yelling, asking if we were just supposed to wait until he shot himself and then bring him in! Something seemed very wrong with the fact that a person was clearly suicidal and not in his right mind, yet they wouldn't admit him.

We got James back to our apartment and finally convinced him to admit himself. He was in the hospital for at least two weeks, but it might have even been longer than that. That's when James was first diagnosed with manic depression, which is the same thing as what we call bipolar today. He was put on medication, and it made a huge, huge difference. He was like a new person. That was really my first eye into mental illness.

After describing my brother's more overt troubles, I also explained that I'd had my own struggles with depression. In my family, I'm the youngest of five. My dad had been an only child, and his mother would smack him upside the head and tell him, "That's for what you might be doing later." So, his upbringing wasn't necessarily the most awesome, which means he didn't have a good example to draw on when he became a parent. That may be why Dad didn't really know how to deal with my two brothers, who caused a lot of trouble. He never hit the girls at all, but he would beat the boys—beat them black and blue.

I have a very vivid childhood memory that has significantly affected me. When my other brother, Luke, was probably sixteen, he came home way after curfew. Plus, I believe he was drunk, and the car might have been wrecked.

Maggie and I, who shared a room as kids, were both just lying in our beds, crying, as we heard Dad go in and start shouting at my brother. Luke was screaming, "Don't, Dad! Please don't," and Mom was yelling, "No, no, stop! Richard, don't!" Then, we heard Dad telling my mom to shut up and go back to bed—and the sounds of fists on flesh.

Now, I wasn't in the room, so I don't know what occurred, but the vision in my head was that Luke was on the sofa and Dad was on top of him punching him. I don't know if that's really how it happened, but I know what I heard, and that, for years, was my most vivid childhood memory.

This impacted me tremendously, and for a long time, I had anger—not only toward my dad but toward my mom too. Like how could you let these things happen? Because this wasn't the only time something like this occurred. For instance, I know that James ran away one time, and Dad found him, brought him home, took him in the garage, and beat him. Basically, it was a pattern . . . My brothers would do something stupid, and my dad would beat them. Like I said, he just didn't know how to deal with the boys.

So, I had struggled for a while. I had seen a therapist and a psychiatrist to try to deal with it more productively. And I'd taken antidepressants, like Wellbutrin, which helped me enormously.

After going over my history, we discussed Rob's mental health background with Dr. Stanley. He has always struggled with depression, ever since I've known him. And at some point, he ended up on this depression medication. He didn't realize at the time—it took probably ten years to see that the medication was having this effect on him—but it caused him to have a very short fuse. Dangerously short.

So, for example, there were times when something minor happened, and he would just blow a gasket. And when I say blow a gasket, I mean flip a kitchen table upside down, break the garage door with his bare hands, punch a hole in the wall. These were things that my kids were witnessing, and it scared them. So, I, on more than one occasion, made it clear I was not going to have my children living in a house where they were afraid like I was growing up.

Luckily, Rob eventually figured out that the medication was causing these violent fits of temper in him, and he was able to switch to something new. Now, he has a totally different temperament, though he does still struggle with his mental health when he forgets to take his medicine or experiences extreme stress.

At this point, Dr. Stanley had a pretty well-rounded understanding of our family's history in terms of mental illness. But when telling her about my brother and the other mental health issues in my family, I told her I did *not* want her to diagnose Katie with bipolar disorder until she had ruled out every other possibility. I didn't want Katie to have to carry the burden of the stigma associated with that diagnosis, especially at such a young age. To my relief, the doctor agreed and prescribed medication for attention-deficit disorder as well as Prozac for depression. We'd hoped that would help, but that didn't turn out to be the case.

LAUREN

Winter 2005

It was a crisp, dry evening, and we wore our jackets unzipped over our jeans and sweatshirts. We were playing outside. Four square. Kind of difficult to do with only two people, but our imaginations were big enough to accommodate this obstacle.

I remember thinking Katie had been acting strange lately, though I can't remember if it had started off slow or happened all at once. All I know is that Mom and Dad were having hushed conversations, and Katie's teachers were calling our home. She wasn't as funny as she used to be either. In fact, sometimes she was downright scary. Her easy laugh had been replaced by brooding glares and sullen pouts. She didn't play with me as often anymore, preferring to spend more time by herself.

I felt a bit lonely.

I had her attention in that moment though. We didn't have a kickball or bouncy ball, so we played four square with a worn basketball. We shoved the ball back and forth, each trying to intimidate the other. I was frustrated that Katie was being so serious.

Her laughter often faded into a scowl, and I wasn't having nearly as much fun as I'd expected.

I was finally able to coax a small smile out of her as I fumbled the ball. Katie became king, and we played Pacman, a mini-game that we either made up or learned from other kids at recess. She was the "ghost," and it was her job to tag me. I shuffled quickly down the line I was standing on, careful not to lose my balance because stepping off the line would automatically make me lose. Katie prowled after me, a determined gleam in her eye. In desperation, I scrambled away even faster, hooking a sharp left at an intersecting line, but it was too late. Katie had grabbed my sleeve, and I had lost.

I sighed and moved to stand back in my square but stopped in my tracks when I saw Katie's face. I'd expected her to look triumphant, a self-satisfied smirk playing across her lips, but her face was dark and empty. Katie appeared to have grown tired of our game; she didn't return to her square but rather wandered along the driveway, looking thoughtful—haunted even.

I watched her for a few moments, my eyebrows knitting together when she occasionally muttered as if talking to someone, though I was the only one around. She had taken to doing that a lot lately.

I wanted to ask her what was wrong, but I was scared. I'd noticed the scratches and bite marks on her arms in recent days. I'd seen her clench both of her hands around her windpipe when angry the week before. I'd overheard my parents whispering about her progressively erratic and harmful behavior. Something was terribly, terribly wrong, and I wasn't sure I was prepared to learn the extent of it. As uneasy as I felt, it seemed much more comfortable to remain in my safe state of oblivion.

But . . . I did already know some things, and those few pieces of the puzzle were tickling the back of my brain, begging to be understood. Plus, I wanted to protect my little sister, the most important person in the world to me. How could I protect her if I didn't know what I was protecting her from?

Feeling nervous, I stepped closer to Katie and took a deep breath. "What are you thinking about?"

She snapped her dead eyes in my direction, and I stumbled backward a bit, alarmed at the expression on her face.

She didn't answer.

Anger shot through me at what I perceived to be a surly silence on her part. Huffing loudly, I lifted my chin and leveled an icy glare in her direction.

She ignored me.

For a moment, I stood there, unsure of what to do next. Finally, just as I was about to turn around and go inside, Katie spoke.

"Do you have imaginary friends?"

"Not really. I have angels."

"Angels?"

"Yeah. A bunch of them. Ruby, Sapphire, Saffron, and Emerald. They watch over me and make me feel better."

Katie nodded. "I have Charlie and Bob." She hesitated. "They watch me all the time too. They don't make me feel better though. They tell me things."

Her answer was unexpected. My angels were made up, of course. I knew there were no such things as imaginary friends. I just wanted to believe that God was watching over me in a personal way.

"Wh-what kinds of things?" I sat down on the cold concrete, my mouth open in awe. I expected her to sit too, but she continued walking around, tracing the grooves in the driveway.

"They tell me to hurt myself."

"Why would they do that?"

"I don't know." For the first time since she'd started talking, she looked up at me, and the fear in her eyes stopped my breath. "They tell me I should hurt people too. You, Sarah, Mommy and Daddy. People at school. The other day, someone was using a game I wanted to play with at indoor recess, and Charlie told me to punch them in the face."

"Did you?" I gasped.

"No, but I wanted to."

"Have you told Mommy and Daddy?"

"I'm afraid to. They keep talking about me. I think they're mad at me. I don't want them to be mad at me again." Tears were streaking hotly down her cheeks now.

"Katie, Mom and Dad aren't going to be mad at you. They just want to help."

"Right now, Bob and Charlie are telling me to run into the middle of the street," said Katie abruptly, looking away again.

"Why would they want you to do that?"

"They want me to get hit by a car."

"What!" I jumped to my feet, incensed. "You don't want to get hit by a car. You would get really hurt. You might die!"

"I know. Sometimes I feel like I want to die."

I didn't know what to say, and she seemed to be done talking. As much as I wanted to run inside and tell Mom and Dad about what Katie had told me, I was reluctant to leave her outside on her own, just in case she *did* decide to jump out in front of cars. We stayed there, leaving each other to our own thoughts, until the sun had almost set, and Mom was calling us in for dinner.

LAUREN

Spring 2005

When Katie was in the first grade and I was in the third grade, we started walking to Jane's house after school. Jane was a kind, strict, elderly woman who lived six houses down the road from our elementary school. We loved going to Jane's house because we got to play with kids our age every single school day while we waited for Mom to get off work. It was like having play-dates five days out of each week.

Other than Katie and me, there were four kids who went to Jane's after school on a regular basis: Dan, David, Ben, and Casie. Dan was the same age as me, but I didn't talk to him too much. I was very shy around boys, and he was pretty shy too. His little brother, David, was Katie's age, and he wasn't shy at all. He was perhaps the bossiest, telling everyone what to do, shouting when things didn't go his way, and cursing at us constantly. (Incidentally, I learned the majority of the curse words I know today from him.) Ben was also Katie's age. He was a bit of a wild card. At times, he could be very sweet and sensitive. At others, he was a bit aggressive and acted more like David.

Casie is Jane's granddaughter; she and her mother and younger sister actually lived with Jane and her husband, Jerry. Casie was the only girl my age who was consistently there. We instantly became best friends and have been close ever since. In fact, Casie is one of the only friends I seek out when Katie is having a hard time. She's been there from the beginning of my family's journey with mental illness, and she continues to be a great comfort to me when things are rough.

Our little crew of six played house, four square, and tag outside. We also made up a game that we cleverly named The Kicking Game. It involved two people swinging on the swings in sync with each other and one person throwing a giant bouncy ball at them. One of the swingers had to kick the ball as far as it would go. We were eventually forbidden from playing The Kicking Game because the grass started to die in the spot where the "pitcher" always stood.

The six of us grew pretty close over the few years we went to Jane's. We were quick to tattle on one another but quick to console one another as well. We were probably as close to a family as a group of kids could manage.

I guess, then, it wasn't the *worst* place for Katie to lose it.

We were playing outside as usual. It was a new kind of game. It essentially involved smacking one another as hard as possible with all the flyswatters Jane had laying around the screened-in back deck. One minute, Katie seemed fine. The next, she was gone.

I went down the stairs leading to the back patio and looked around for her. She was sulking by herself halfway underneath the stairs.

"What are you doing?"

She glared at me. It looked like she had scratch marks on her exposed arms. I didn't know whether to be angry or scared.

"What's up?" asked Casie from behind me. She'd gotten bored of whacking David and Dan and decided to check out what was going on with us.

"I have no idea."

All of a sudden, Katie leapt up, her eyes ablaze and her fists clenched. Casie and I each took a step back, completely alarmed.

"I hate you! I hate you!" she bellowed, raising her fists. Then, to our astonishment, she started choking herself.

Now that I'm older, I know that her behavior was mostly harmless. She could choke herself until she passed out, but then her hands would relax, and she would breathe again. She certainly wouldn't die. However, at the time, I was only eleven years old, and I thought she was going to strangle herself to death. In a state of panic, I launched forward and grabbed at her hands, scrabbling my nails against her tight fingers, watching in horror as her face turned redder and redder.

"Stop it, Katie! Stop!" I screamed, yanking on her wrists. A few times, I managed to pull a hand away from her throat, but almost immediately, she would snatch it sharply away and clench it around her windpipe again.

"Please, please, please," I groaned, tears streaming down my cheeks as I settled for kicking Katie in the shins. "Why are you doing this?"

Casie, who had been rooted to the spot when Katie initially started choking herself, finally snapped out of it enough to race upstairs to go inside and find Jane. Before Jane could come out though, Katie relaxed her hands and let them fall to her sides. We both sat down side by side on the edge of the patio, panting. Red lines stood out against the pale skin of her neck as her pulse fluttered frantically at the base of her throat.

MOM

Spring 2005

Katie would frequently have meltdowns that made no sense. For example, on Martin Luther King Jr. Day, I took the girls to the local roller rink to skate. Their elementary school had a family night there that evening, and I thought the girls would want to skate with their friends. When I returned about an hour later to take them home, Katie was sitting on the floor, crying and kicking her feet because she couldn't get her skates off. I understand becoming frustrated, but this was over the top—a complete meltdown.

She would also have problems every time we went out to dinner. I like going out to eat, so I would always forget what a stressful experience it was until we got there. Katie wouldn't be able to sit still, so I would have to get up and walk around with her to calm her down.

One time, I thought it would be fun to take the Amtrak from Kirkwood to Washington, Missouri, to have dinner and then take the train back. It was only a forty-five-minute trip in each direction, and I figured the girls would think it was fun to ride the train.

When we got to Washington, we found a cute little restaurant and ordered our food. As always, Katie began to get very anxious and couldn't sit still. Not long after, she was crying at the table. I took her outside and walked around with her, and then Rob and I took turns going outside so we could each eat our dinner. We learned that night that the only thing worse than Katie having a meltdown while we were out to dinner was Katie having a meltdown while we were out to dinner . . . *and* us having to wait for a train to come and take us back home!

In addition, Katie continued to act up and have issues at school. All too often, the counselor would call me at work, and I would have to pick Katie up and bring her home. This was happening several times a week! Sometimes she could calm down enough to go back to class if I just came and wandered around or sat with her. More often than not, however, I would need to take her home.

A contributing factor to Katie's constant breakdowns at school was Mrs. Karol's student teacher, who was becoming more active in the classroom. Her name was Ms. Wiley, and Katie did not like her at all. She was adamant that Ms. Wiley hated her, and there was no convincing her of anything different. But when we would talk to Mrs. Karol about it, she would say that it was absolutely not true and that Ms. Wiley would try extra hard with Katie to help her feel better about it.

Katie didn't just have meltdowns while in school. She tended to have problems whenever she was away from me and Rob in general. Inevitably, if I was going out with a friend or with my sisters, Katie would have a crisis, and I'd have to cancel my plans. And Rob and I weren't able to go out just the two of us because there was always a lot of chaos. We usually just didn't feel comfortable that everything was going to be okay at home without us there.

Eventually, once Katie grew up a bit, we would decide to work on us and have our date nights on a regular basis. We would realize how important it is to take care of ourselves even as we take care of our children—particularly our child with mental health challenges. But back when Katie was in the early stages of her mental illness journey, we tended to forgo as many social opportunities as we could.

In March, Rob and I were scheduled to go on my work trip, something I was worried about, considering how often Katie needed me to come up to school. Since it was for work, there was no way to get out of it. Besides, in spite of my worries, I knew the trip would be fun in different circumstances.

I clearly remember sitting in my parents' family room, crying and thanking them for keeping the girls for the week. I knew it would be a lot to handle because Lauren and Katie fought so often, and Katie was still struggling. (Sarah was too little to be involved in conflicts with her sisters—for the time being.) I prayed that Katie would be okay for my parents! Rob and I really needed a break from all of it.

Luckily, Mrs. Karol was so great while we were gone! She emailed me each day to let me know how Katie was doing and assure me that everything was going okay. I really appreciated that contact because I was constantly concerned about how Katie was getting along without having me to come sit with her when she started having problems.

Unfortunately, overall, it seemed that things were getting worse instead of improving. So, we continued to see Dr. Stanley every week, hoping against hope that something would change, and Katie would start to feel better.

LAUREN

Spring 2005

Katie had smiled maybe twice in the past hour. We were at a pottery painting place for a birthday party, and our masterpieces had just gone into the kiln. Caroline, our babysitter, had a gentle hand on Katie's shoulder.

"All right, guys. Are you ready to go home?"

Katie scowled.

"Yes," I murmured, annoyed that Katie was being such a brat.

Caroline smiled sweetly and led us out the door, her long, blonde bob swaying with her movements. We walked to the car quietly. Caroline opened the back, and I slid in right away, always obedient. Katie didn't.

"No."

"Come on, Katie. Let's go home so we can play Monopoly."

"No. I want to get smoothies."

Caroline glanced up at Smoothie Planet, located two doors down from The Painted Pot. "No, Katie. Like I said earlier, I told you I would take you there if you guys didn't fight . . . but you *did* fight. So, we're not getting smoothies."

"No!" Katie shrieked, fists balled at her sides, her face screwed up in outrage.

"Let's be a good listener, okay? How about we go home and play Monopoly like we talked about. You can be the dog if you want."

"No."

My car door was still open. I watched from the back seat, embarrassed, as Caroline tried to coax Katie into the car to no avail. Katie only seemed to grow more and more furious with each word Caroline spoke.

Suddenly, Katie stormed over to the front of the car. Her fingernails were biting so hard into her palms that I was afraid she was going to hurt herself. Her face was bright red, but her eyes were no longer slitted. Quite suddenly, they looked almost devoid of emotion altogether.

"Hit me," she challenged, voice dangerously low. "Drive. Hit me with your car."

Caroline gaped at her, unsure how to respond for a second.

"Get in the car, Katie," I shouted, finally fed up. Her eyes snapped to me, but she didn't move or speak. "Don't be stupid. Get in the car NOW."

"NO!" she screamed, and now tears were in her eyes. She crouched down so it would be harder to move her by force. "I want to get hit by a car. I want to."

"What are you talking about, Katie? That's crazy."

"Come on, hon. Why are you saying that?" asked Caroline, who was understandably unnerved by Katie's behavior.

Abruptly, Katie leapt up and started walking toward Clayton Road, which was busy with traffic, as always.

"Get her!" I yelled, but Caroline had already grabbed Katie and pulled her toward the car. I expected more of a fight, but Katie just shut down. Caroline struggled to get her into the seat and buckled, but at least Katie didn't try to run away again. She stewed quietly, angry tears wetting the pink collar of her shirt.

When we got home, I went straight to my room, hoping to avoid Katie for a while. I grabbed my *Harry Potter* book and lay on my stomach on my bed . . .

I was abruptly roused back to reality by the sound of a loud admonishment coming from the front of the house. I put my book aside and warily made my way toward the family room.

The babysitter was standing on the threshold between the family room and the kitchen, looking nonplussed. I could tell she was surreptitiously reaching for the phone, afraid any quick motion would send Katie into action. My parents hadn't told Caroline exactly what had been going on with Katie, but the knife in Katie's hands gave her a pretty good indication.

I ducked past Caroline and walked briskly toward my little sister, my eyes widening with alarm. Caroline took that opportunity to grab our home phone off the hook on the counter. I heard her start dialing as she strode into the other room.

Katie sat on the counter in the kitchen, eyes blank, mouth tight, staring intensely at the knife in her hands. She turned the sharp instrument over and over, paying no mind to me as I hauled myself up onto the yellow Formica counter beside her.

"Katie?" I asked hesitantly. She neither responded nor looked up at me. "Can you please stop playing with that knife?" I pleaded with her, unnerved by her behavior and apparent lack of emotion.

For a long moment, she ignored me. Then, unexpectedly, she whipped her head around to gaze at me with hard eyes. With an unshaking hand, she held the knife to her neck.

"You want me to, don't you?" she whispered harshly. "You want me to do it. You would like it if I killed myself, wouldn't you?"

"No!" I sobbed, startled. Horrified tears splashed onto my shirt. "No, I would never want that!"

"You do—you want that. I know you do. It would make you happy if I killed myself."

"No. Please—I don't want that."

"I know you do," she spat, launching herself to the tile floor and hurling the knife at the counter. I scrambled out of the way of the glinting blade as she stalked from the room.

I was overcome by a fog of shock and guilt. Katie and I fought frequently and spat spiteful comments at each other all the time, but I had never, ever felt the desire for her to be gone from my life. As much of a brat as she was sometimes, she was my best friend. Not only that, but she was my little sister. Even as an eleven-year-old girl, I knew that I would do anything to protect her. The last thing I wanted was for her to get hurt.

This conversation, which Katie only faintly remembers, still haunts me. It is possibly the most vivid memory I have. I'll never forget the look on her face or the words she said to me as she stroked that knife. I'll never be rid of the guilt that settled onto my heart that night. Even now, when Katie loses control and self-harms (something that, fortunately, hasn't happened for a long time), I automatically blame myself. I can't escape the cumbersome feeling that she hurt herself because she believed I wanted her to. I didn't tell her I love her often enough. I didn't spend enough time with her. I didn't make her feel important.

I wasn't a good big sister.

Mom and Dad came home within twenty minutes of the babysitter's phone call, but I was already holed up in my room, curled up in my bed, fighting to find sleep.

MOM

Spring 2005

By April, things had spiraled even further downhill, and we'd reached a breaking point. I received a call from the school counselor, who told me I needed to come pick Katie up and take her to the emergency room. As I soon discovered, Katie had asked the kids in her classroom if they thought you went to heaven or hell if you committed suicide. Then, while the kids were lined up in the hallway, waiting to go to choir, Katie had announced that she wouldn't be at school the next day because she was going to set her alarm for the middle of the night and cut her throat.

"This is actually a plan," the counselor told me. "You have to take this seriously."

Terrified and distraught, I took the counselor's advice. Rushing out of my office, I picked Katie up from school and took her to the emergency room. On the way there, I called Dr. Stanley to let her know what was going on. It was only then that I found out she didn't have any hospital privileges. This was something that I never in my wildest dreams would have thought I'd have to check into when looking for a psychiatrist for my daughter. In fact, I never would have thought I'd be taking my daughter to the emergency room for this at all!

Dr. Stanley told me to take Katie to what is now Mercy Hospital and gave me her cell phone number, telling me to call and let her know what was going on. But she made it abundantly clear that I was only to call to give her updates—then, I was never again to use that number. I was completely annoyed! I'm in the middle of a crisis, and you're worried I might bother you on your cell phone?

At the emergency room, they did a psychological evaluation and told us that if we thought we could keep Katie safe, we could take her home. Then, she could begin an intensive outpatient program (IOP) the next day. We felt we *could* keep her safe, so we went home, and I had her sleep on the floor in my room—right next to my bed. We also removed anything we thought she could hurt herself with. We definitely did not have a very restful sleep that night!

DAD

Spring 2005

I don't have a particular first memory associated with Katie's mental illness. I do recall taking Lauren to see a child psychologist in 2002 because we were concerned about her preference for reading rather than playing with friends during recess. While we were dealing with that, Ms. Danvers, Katie's kindergarten teacher, told us that Katie had become very sad. At that point, we had the psychologist see both Katie and Lauren. (Even back then, Katie was squeezing in on Lauren and her issues.) We didn't seem to get anywhere with either of our girls with the psychologist, so we didn't continue with it for more than a couple of months.

It was roughly three years later that things with Katie resurfaced, and we took her to see Dr. Stanley. I remember being irritated that it was so difficult to find a child psychiatrist that we were forced to go to someone who didn't accept any insurance. Dr. Stanley put Katie on an antidepressant. Then, after a period of time, Anne was contacted by Mrs. Karol, who indicated that Katie had told her classmates she would not be there the following day, as she was going to wake up early and kill herself by slitting her throat.

Most of the above are things that I know occurred, but to be honest, I don't have specific memories of them. The first real memory I have is being at Mercy in the admissions department that evening, speaking with their intake folks. I recall being surrounded by orange and gold fabric on the dividers and chairs, reminding me of the outdated decor from when I worked at aerospace manufacturing corporation McDonnell Douglas.

The lady from intake sat behind a modern, light oak desk and told us that we should put Katie into their inpatient unit. I looked to my left to see Anne had tears running down her face. Katie was sitting in her lap, and Anne had her arms around her as though she thought someone might take Katie away from us. It seemed so surreal. I couldn't get my head around it all. I mean, what could an eight-year-old be experiencing that would lead to her to consider suicide? I suppose I was in denial at a certain level, thinking this was just Katie acting out some melodramatic story.

Anne didn't want to leave Katie even though that's really why we went to the hospital to begin with. Ultimately, Anne decided we would take her home with us and keep a close eye on her while returning each day for Katie to attend IOP. I remember the woman from intake repeatedly asking if we were absolutely sure that we could keep Katie safe. We insisted we could. I hoped that was true and that we were doing the right thing.

MOM

Spring 2005

The IOP program was located in a separate building on the hospital campus. The morning after the alarm clock incident at school, I dropped Katie off at eight o'clock, hoping the day would go well. When I picked her up at two in the afternoon, I met with the IOP psychiatrist, Dr. Bandi.

After getting all the background information, she immediately indicated her belief that Katie has bipolar. However, she would not give that diagnosis officially because Katie was too young to have truly exhibited any of the high highs and low lows. Plus, she didn't want to put that stigma on her at such an early age. As much as I didn't want that diagnosis, I was relieved that we now knew what was wrong and could work to manage the illness.

As it turns out, if you have bipolar and you're put on just an antidepressant, it can actually make things worse. So, instead of making her better, the Prozac had actually had the opposite effect. Katie never should have taken it!

If I'd known then what I know now, I would not have been worried about the stigma at all. Not only would that have helped us understand Katie's situation better, but it would have also reinforced what I truly believe: there is no shame in having a mental illness, and there is no shame in having bipolar disorder. In fact, after everything our family's been through, I feel it's almost my mission in life to help eradicate the stigma associated with mental illness because we should be able to talk about it as freely as we talk about heart disease and diabetes. So, I do wish I hadn't insisted on Dr. Stanley overlooking a bipolar diagnosis—and not just because it made Katie's condition worse for a while.

Dr. Bandi took Katie off the Prozac and started her on some new medications. I don't remember everything they put her on, but I do recall she took Seroquel. She was also put on Lamictal, which really seemed to work for her.

Now, as great as these medications were for Katie's mental health, one of the unfortunate side effects disrupted her physically. When Katie started taking these medications, they made her very, very hungry. So, Katie experienced some weight gain, which I'm sure was hard for her to deal with on top of everything else going on. Her distress over these side effects may have slowed her recovery somewhat, though she did start improving steadily. And, of course, despite Katie's concerns, she was a beautiful and healthy little girl!

I really liked Dr. Bandi, so we decided that we wanted Katie to see her instead of Dr. Stanley. She was very hesitant because within the doctor community, it's taboo for one doctor to take away another doctor's patient. (At least, that was my understanding.) But we made it clear that we were not going back to Dr. Stanley because she was not in our network, and she didn't have hospital privileges. So, we were changing anyway, and we wanted to change to Dr. Bandi. In the end, she agreed.

At the same time, we decided to find a new therapist for Katie as well. I asked one of Katie's nurses at IOP who she would recommend, and she suggested someone named Brea. We immediately called to schedule the appointment.

After going to IOP for two weeks, Katie started transitioning back to school. She would go to IOP three days a week and school two days a week. We did that for two more weeks before she was officially released from IOP.

One of the most beneficial aspects of IOP for Katie was that she learned strategies for managing her mental illness. Coping skills for an eight-year-old are a bit different from an adult's. They include screaming into your pillow or punching it when you're angry, coloring when you're sad or lonely, and using a stress ball when you're anxious or nervous. These are very basic skills that a child can understand, and they tend to be fairly effective—if you use them. Katie wasn't quite ready to actually apply these coping skills on a regular basis, but it was a start.

During that time frame, Katie had her first appointment with Brea, and the two of them just clicked. Brea was young, pretty, and nice, and I think that helped Katie connect with her so well. This, along with the treatment she received at IOP, helped her stabilize. She still definitely had her moments, but life did seem to calm down a bit.

LAUREN

Spring 2005

I sat quietly in the back seat, watching dully as houses and cars flashed by my window. I had become near-silent since The Incident and its ensuing consequences.

About a week before, Katie had started asking her classmates whether they thought people who committed suicide went to hell. Her teacher, Mrs. Karol, was obviously very concerned, considering they were all only in the third grade. As bad as that was, things got much worse. Later that day, Katie announced to her class that she was planning on setting her alarm clock that night and slashing her throat. At that point, my parents were called, and it wasn't long before Katie was at the hospital.

She had been going to IOP for a few days before I had to come along to pick her up. Katie's absence didn't directly affect my day since we were in different grades. However, throughout each day, I was all too aware that she wasn't just across the building from me. Instead of acknowledging my sadness and confusion, I pretended that it wasn't real and avoided talking about it altogether.

Unfortunately, I couldn't remain in denial for much longer; I would be seeing Katie in the outpatient setting in just a few minutes.

Cold, gray light shone from the pearly sky. I gazed up at the suffocating clouds and prayed to God that Katie would be okay and that I would be strong enough. For the rest of the drive, I stared up at the overcast sky because it made me feel like God was holding my hand.

I finally looked around when my mom parked the car in a mostly empty parking lot. Although I was eleven years old and capable of walking across a parking lot on my own, I allowed my mom to take my hand as we went down several stairs and across a walkway covered by a long, blue awning. After signing in with the lady at the front desk, Mom led me to an elevator, and I climbed on, feeling more and more nervous by the minute. I had no idea what I was about to see.

When we got off at the second floor, Mom steered me to a large wooden door. It was locked. She knocked and waited restlessly for someone to let us in. I almost hoped the door would stay closed. I wanted Katie to be at home, waiting to play with me. Not behind that door.

Finally, someone opened the door for us, careful not to let any wayward children sneak out. Mom approached the desk and talked to the nurses. I shrank against her, completely overwhelmed.

My first thought was that Katie didn't belong here. She was too funny, too full of life, too normal to be here. Later, I would realize that those kids were probably just as normal as Katie. I would realize that they were brothers and sisters and sons and daughters. I would realize that they, too, were human beings who'd just lost control of themselves. I would feel ashamed of myself for looking upon them with fear and revulsion. At that moment, uneducated and inexperienced as I was, I bought into the same stigma that I seek to eliminate today. I thought that the children looked crazy.

It was a strange mixture of bedlam and tedium. Some boys and girls chased one another around, clearly full of an enormous amount of energy. One of the nurses at the desk admonished them for being so rowdy. A few other children were sprawled out in chairs, looking bored. I could tell they were tired of being stuck in the hospital. One boy with wide, empty eyes had drool sparkling on his face, but he seemed oblivious to it. A tall African American boy was wrapped up in a blue blanket, rocking backward and forward and staring at nothing. I thought I heard him muttering under his breath, but maybe it was my imagination.

A girl with a bowl cut and a striped turtleneck ran over to us at the desk and began spouting nonsense words at us. She tugged repeatedly at her shirt, shifted excitedly from foot to foot, and laughed raucously at apparently nothing. I clutched even closer to my mother, terrified that my sister was surrounded by these people (though, looking back, most of them seemed like average kids).

Katie suddenly appeared, acting like she was in charge, as usual. "Hey! Boundaries," she said snottily to the babbling girl. Instead of being deterred, the girl simply grinned bigger and jabbered even louder. "She is so annoying," groaned Katie, rolling her eyes. "She thinks we are best friends."

"Come on, girls," said Mom, putting a hand out for each of us and gently pulling us out the door, which was held open for us by a nurse. "How was your day, Katie?"

"It was good," replied Katie carelessly. "I got really mad when Kelsey kept following me around, but I was able to calm down."

"I heard about that," frowned Mom. "Did you practice the coping skills Dr. Bandi taught you about?"

"I tried," whined Katie, "but they don't even work that much."

Mom sighed. I glanced at Katie out of the corner of my eye and felt hope flutter inside of me. Katie wasn't back to herself yet, but she seemed to be on her way. With the new medicine she was taking and the extra therapy she was getting at IOP, the bad moments seemed to be occurring slightly less frequently.

The ground looked a little bit wet when we stepped out from under the awning. I wondered if it had rained briefly while we were inside. I looked up at the sky and pressed my hands together for a moment.

"Thank you, God," I whispered as I yanked open the car door and settled myself into the seat next to Katie, who chattered the whole ride home.

MOM

Spring 2005

When Katie was (unofficially) diagnosed with bipolar, I immediately went to the bookstore. I was basically starved for information, so I wanted to educate myself and find out as much as I could. Unfortunately, there weren't many books out there that talked about mental illness with children. At that time, the books all talked about mental illness in adults.

The problem is bipolar presents itself very differently in children compared to adults. As you can imagine, if you're eight years old and you have bipolar, you're not going out on shopping sprees and engaging in promiscuous or risky behavior. That's not how that works at eight. But that may be what you do when you're an adult. So, these books didn't provide much useful insight for my particular situation. Nonetheless, I bought some of them and read them just in case. I figured some information was better than none.

Now, someone did recommend *The Bipolar Child* to me, which *was* very helpful. In fact, I still have the book with all my highlights and sticky notes all over. It was, without a doubt, the best resource

I was able to find in terms of books on childhood bipolar! In my opinion, it helped to see symptoms and experiences in writing and be able to say, "Yeah, I see that in my child" or "Ooh, no, I don't see that one so much."

You see, it's not like a doctor can do a blood test and say, "Your kid has this!" It's based on what you see as a parent and what you're telling the doctor. So, you basically have to put your trust in the psychiatrist and hope that their diagnosis is accurate. Of course, you can never be 100 percent sure, but reading information like what I discovered in *The Bipolar Child* can help you make connections and feel more confident in the diagnosis. And that can make you feel a lot better about the measures being taken to help your child fight their mental illness.

LAUREN

Summer 2005

It's hard to explain the aftermath of the first time Katie's mental illness made itself stridently, unmistakably known. After a couple of weeks, Katie had recovered enough to stop going to IOP, though she continued to take medication. She had stopped jumping in front of cars, carving into her skin with paper clips, and threatening to slit her own throat anyway. This was obviously a vast improvement.

But she was different.

She was . . . quiet. Withdrawn. Simmering with self-loathing and unhappiness. She was stable but shaky all at once. There were many—too many—days when she wanted to hurt herself, wanted to die.

All sense of security was lost for Katie. She followed my mom around, afraid to leave her sight. Going to school was a fight every day. She rarely laughed, rarely even smiled—at least compared to before. She had always been my best friend, but suddenly, she was a stranger. We barely talked at all for a while.

Katie seemed only a whisper of her old self. Her silence frightened me. I longed to know what she was thinking, but I was too afraid to ask.

In spite of this, Katie was finally able to return to a fairly normal way of living. Even when she sank into a depression or soared into a manic state, she was mostly functional. Like other nine-year-olds, she went to school, played with friends, even had a little "boyfriend." All seemed well, at least relatively.

Unfortunately, though she certainly hadn't done anything wrong, the memories of her struggles with mental illness filled her with shame and embarrassment. This hugely impacted her relationships with others. Katie and I drifted away from each other to a certain extent as I entered middle school and spent more time with friends. She eventually broke up with her "boyfriend," in part because she was afraid he would find out what had happened with her. Within a few years, she and her dear friend Anna were no longer close. Katie seemed heartbroken and alone, quailing at the lingering specter of her mental illness.

MOM

Spring 2006

It was a fairly nice spring day. As I drove to work, I noticed that the flowers were starting to sprout up. We were still struggling with Katie, so noticing the flowers was a nice distraction.

I was the sales manager for a large insurance company, and my office comprised me and one other person. I was always thankful I had considerable flexibility during this time because I was getting a lot of phone calls from school and frequently needed to go up there to talk with teachers. But I still had a job to do. To make up for these workday interruptions, I worked extra hard while in the office and frequently did work in the evenings and on weekends to make sure everything got done.

When I arrived at work on that beautiful day, I went to my office to turn on my computer. Then, as I did every day, I went to the breakroom to get hot water for my tea. On my way back to my workspace, I stopped to say good morning to Marla, the account manager who worked with me.

"Hey there! How's it going?"

She looked up from what she was working on and smiled. "Good morning! How's Katie doing?"

"Things are still pretty rough . . ."

Marla was a great source of support for me. She was always there to listen when I needed to talk . . . and I talked a lot because that was how I coped with things.

After chatting for a while, I went back to my office to begin my day. But by 9:30 a.m., my phone was ringing. The caller ID told me it was school. My heart sank. *Not already.*

It was the school counselor, Mrs. Norman.

"Good morning. What's going on?" I asked, trying to tamp down the anxiety in my voice.

"Katie's having a meltdown and struggling with anxiety. She asked me to call you . . . I hope that's okay."

"Of course," I sighed, then asked her to put Katie on the phone.

"Mommy, I don't know what's wrong," Katie sobbed. "I'm having bad thoughts. I can't sit still."

"Would it help if I came up and sat with you for a few minutes?" I asked gently.

"Yes, b-but I feel bad making you come here."

"Not a problem, sweetheart. I'll be there shortly."

This wasn't a rare occurrence. Actually, it's still pretty common, even though Katie is a grown adult now and is very good at managing her mental illness on her own. The reality is Katie has always been very attached to me, and she often experienced separation anxiety when I wasn't with her. So, Katie's struggle with mental illness has brought the two of us together and made us very close. I've tended to be the person who Katie comes to when she's having an issue, and I'm the one who can almost always make her feel better. Ever since Katie started having a hard time, that's been my role.

While I value our close relationship, we have been told there's some codependency. In other words, she depends on me too much, and I guess I *let* her depend on me. Although, if you have a distraught child who wants to sit with you in the car for ten minutes, and you know that could make her feel better, what mother wouldn't do that? It's kind of a hard balance to keep, and I'm always riding that line between doing everything possible to keep my daughter safe and stable and letting her figure it out on her own and grow more self-sufficient.

Regardless, I think that our relationship is very strong because I am the person she knows she can come to. She knows that no matter what she does, even though I might get angry, I do always still love her. Though her mental illness makes her doubt it sometimes, she knows in her heart that I will always be there for her and will never give up on her. And that's why, starting at such a young age, Katie was so insistent on me being the one to come up to school and sit with her.

As I drove to the elementary school, I was no longer noticing the blossoming flowers. My mind was completely focused on Katie and trying to figure out what was going on. How were things going to get better?

I pulled into the parking lot at school. As usual, all the spots were filled with cars. So, I just pulled up in the bus lane and parked there, hoping I wouldn't get into any trouble. Then, walking swiftly, I went into the front office to sign in.

"Good morning," greeted Mrs. Butterfield and Mrs. Marin in unison. By this time, everyone knew me pretty well!

"Mrs. Norman is expecting me," I sighed.

"You can go on down to her office," said Mrs. Marin with a sympathetic smile.

Moments later, I was striding into Mrs. Norman's office. Poor Katie was sitting in a chair crying, and I immediately went over and hugged her.

"Is it okay if I take her outside for a walk?" I asked.

"No problem at all. I'll be here when you get back."

I had begun to realize that doing things that would distract Katie's "bad" thoughts was very helpful. I thought a walk outside would be an effective distraction since it was such a nice day. So, Katie and I meandered around for about ten minutes.

"What sounds good for dinner tonight?" I inquired, trying to shift her thoughts.

"Macaroni and cheese!"

"Mac and cheese it is then," I smiled. "Do you think you can go back to class and make it through the rest of your day?"

"I think so."

"Great! Let's go back in and get you back to class. But if you need anything, you can always call me, okay?" I think just knowing that she could call if she needed to was a comfort to her.

We walked back into the building hand in hand. As we approached Mrs. Norman's office, Katie started squeezing my hand just a little harder. "It's going to be fine," I told her. "You can do this, Katie. I know you can."

As Katie walked back to class with Mrs. Norman, I headed back down the hallway to leave the building. As I drove away, I was overcome with exhaustion. I felt immensely emotional and frustrated. Why couldn't we get things fixed and back to normal? Little did I know we were going to need to adjust to a new normal. Things would never be the same as they had been again.

LAUREN

Winter 2007

It was difficult being the older sister of a child living with mental illness. My parents were so caught up with Katie that they no longer had a lot of time for me. They loved me, but Katie demanded so much attention that there wasn't much left to spread around. Any remaining time they had was allotted for my youngest sister, Sarah, because she was so little and needed them more than I did. I understood, but I grew to resent my perceived abandonment. Katie and Sarah may have needed my parents more, but that didn't mean I didn't need them too.

When I was in middle school, I was invited to audition to model for a dance magazine. I was ecstatic! I immediately showed the letter to my mom, dancing around, grinning from ear to ear. Chuckling at my excitement, she took a picture of me posing in my favorite green leotard and tan tights to send in. Then, she put the date of the audition in her calendar.

When the day finally came, I got up earlier than usual, too excited to sleep. I showered, did my hair, and even put on a little bit of makeup. Then, I waltzed to the kitchen to make myself breakfast.

It was pandemonium. Katie was crying and clutching at her cheeks. Her face was all red, except for the pale half-moons etched into her skin from her fingernails. Both my mom and dad were trying to console her, but she wouldn't calm down.

No one took the slightest notice of me.

I went back to my room without breakfast, an ominous feeling hanging over me. As usual, no one came to check on me. The time of my audition came and went. My mom had forgotten all about it. I cried into my pillow, not wanting to draw attention to myself. The last thing I wanted was to make my mom feel bad. I knew Katie needed both my parents' undivided attention, but the disappointment was still crushing.

There were times when the lack of attention I received from my family was crippling to my emotional state. I was transitioning from elementary school to middle school, making my first real group of friends, learning how to wear makeup and flirt with boys. These were incredibly formative years for me, yet I felt like I was on my own a lot of the time.

Sometimes I would talk to my mom about the hardships that I experienced as a girl about to enter her teenage years, but I always felt ashamed because I knew that my problems were nothing compared to Katie's. I knew I needed attention at times, but I didn't feel that I deserved it.

Then, since I wasn't getting the support I needed from my family, I turned away from them and leaned heavily on my friends. However, my concern about Katie's mental health was a pretty weighty topic for eleven-, twelve-, thirteen-year-olds. And since I'd felt so starved for attention for so long, I clung on a little too tightly, which scared people away. So, I ended up going through friends pretty fast and learned fairly quickly that it was a bad idea to be so dependent on others.

Eventually, I took up the tactic of simply shutting my emotions down before I could really feel them. If I cried, it was by myself in my room. Usually, I didn't even let myself cry at all. I couldn't burden others with my problems—not even myself.

In spite of this, I was resilient. The loneliness was suffocating sometimes, but I grew to be self-sufficient, independent, and stronger than ever before. In a way, I like to think I held my family together with my calmness and solidity. I made things easier. My role in the family may have been wearing on me, but it gave me a sense of purpose, and I took it very seriously.

Today, I look back on this feeling of abandonment with ambivalence. On the one hand, I still feel a little hurt that my family didn't make time for me when I needed it the most. On the other hand, I realize that growing up without as much guidance has allowed me to cultivate strength and independence. This is what made it possible for me to excel in school, get involved in service and extracurricular activities, and form friendships with people from all walks of life. I wouldn't be the same person that I am today without those experiences with my family.

My mom never remembered that she was supposed to take me to that audition. She only realized what had happened years later when I told her the story—when the pain of being forgotten didn't sting so much anymore.

MOM

With all the turmoil and fear we were experiencing, many people in our life probably wondered how Rob and I managed to keep Katie safe, raise our family of three children, and keep our marriage intact. Fortunately, although we certainly struggled, our marriage never really suffered.

Rob and I don't have a perfect marriage, of course. There's no such thing. And everything going on with Katie definitely put a strain on our family. But it never really jeopardized our marriage. In fact, I think it brought Rob and me closer together and continued to do so over time.

In my opinion, something like raising a child with a mental illness either makes you stronger or tears you apart. Because Rob and I were able to communicate and commiserate effectively with each other right from the start, Katie's challenges ended up making us stronger.

Based on my experiences, when it comes to maintaining a healthy marriage while raising a child with mental illness, communication is the biggest thing. Talk to each other. Listen to each other. Keep an open mind when you're sharing opinions. Don't just shut your partner down because you think, *Oh, no, I don't think that's right or good.*

It's critical to stay on the same page and be an advocate, not only for your child but for each other. You have to be there and support each other in addition to your child because *you need that support as well.* And nobody understands what's going on inside your house more than your spouse because they're living it too.

So, the communication part is crucial. If you want to become stronger rather than fall apart, both partners have to commit to having that open and honest communication and attitude of working together to overcome the obstacle of mental illness.

DAD

Spring 2008

It was an early spring morning, and Katie and I were headed to Warrenton for a softball tournament. We were scheduled to play the first game of the tournament, so we had to leave the house by six o'clock. It was particularly cold that morning, and I could see my breath as we loaded up the car. Katie and I were going alone as Anne had other commitments.

Katie was never happy about getting up for these early morning games, and that morning was no exception. I no longer recall what triggered her angst and frustration that particular day, but as was often the case, my impatience likely played a factor.

The ballfields were directly across the street from the public high school where we parked our car. As usual, we got out of the vehicle and started to unload her gear. The next thing I clearly remember was my daughter lying on the ground, having a complete meltdown. I tried to get her to calm down and relax without success.

"If there's anything I'm good at, it's relaxing," I told her. "Take some deep breaths and clear your mind."

She reacted as though I had thrown salt into an open wound. I could see the other parents just across the street and thought to myself, *How can I possibly keep this from them when they can easily see for themselves that something is terribly wrong?*

At this point, I was at my wits' end and began to have a breakdown of my own. Not knowing what else to do, I called Anne on the phone. I remember feeling like a complete and utter failure. Anne had other plans, and because I wasn't competent to handle this by myself, I was once again turning to my wife to make things right. To be fair, Anne was the only one who really knew how to calm Katie down, but I wasn't inclined to cut myself any slack at that point.

By the time Anne answered the phone, I was nearly in tears myself and repeating, "I'm so sorry . . . I'm so sorry." I seemed so distraught that Anne immediately became alarmed, wanting to know what was wrong. I think she was actually relieved when I told her what was going on. With Anne's soothing voice in my ear, I was soon able to pull myself together and handed the phone to Katie. Before long, Katie was also feeling better and gaining control of herself.

A big part of Katie pulling herself together was Anne's promise that she was getting herself ready and would soon be heading to the ballfields to watch Katie's games. Whatever plans Anne had made would once again have to be canceled in order to accommodate Katie's mood. Meanwhile, I had to provide some sort of explanation to the other parents.

At this point, we had been dealing with Katie's mental health struggles for roughly three years. Throughout that time, I had never felt my daughter was any less because of her illness, never felt embarrassed or ashamed of it. But now, for the first time, I was actually going to have to discuss it with someone who was neither a loving family member nor a medical professional providing treatment.

How would they see my daughter? Would they look at her differently? Would they treat her differently? How could they not after seeing her rolling on the ground, seemingly out of control? As her father, I couldn't bear to see the expressions of disapproval, the looks of disdain that I knew might be forthcoming. Mind you, I wasn't concerned for myself but for my little girl who hadn't asked for this and surely didn't deserve it.

Recognizing that delaying wasn't going to make it any easier, I resigned myself to the task ahead. Steeling myself, I walked across the street to where the parents were congregating in a few different groups under a large oak tree with a green vine running up the side, trying to stay shaded. I approached the coach and assistant coach, who were standing together.

"I'm betting you're wondering what all that was about." I laughed nervously.

"Is Katie okay?" they asked, clearly concerned.

"Yes, she's all right." Then, taking a deep breath, I jumped in with both feet. Though I found myself becoming emotional, I forced myself to keep going. I began to explain that Katie struggles with mental health challenges, specifically bipolar. To my surprise, I was greeted with genuine concern for my daughter instead of the blank stares—or worse—that I had anticipated. Both expressed empathy and asked what they might do as coaches to make things better. Filled with relief, I explained that they didn't need to do anything—I just felt it was important for them to be aware of it.

Encouraged, I next approached a large group of parents and again began to explain Katie's diagnosis. Once again, I was met with incredible kindness from the other parents. If any of them were passing judgment, they were exceedingly adept at hiding it. All I saw in everyone's eyes was genuine understanding and concern for my daughter and my family. One by one, I approached different groups until I had shared Katie's diagnosis with them. And one by one, they continued to amaze me with their thoughtfulness and consideration.

Finally, I had only one person left with which to speak, but I was particularly uneasy about sharing Katie's challenges with him. He was a nice enough fellow but a little rough around the edges. He had a scraggly beard and was almost never without a lit cigarette in his hand. I had always gotten along with him fine, but I just couldn't picture him being understanding like the other parents. Nevertheless, knowing what had to be done, I walked up to him and started to tell him about Katie.

Even with the kindness that the other parents had shown, I was stunned by his reaction. He reached out, placed his left hand on my shoulder, and told me how sorry he was to hear that Katie had to deal with this. Then, he started to share that he had a very close friend who had bipolar and indicated he knew what a challenge it could be. Before we parted, he made it clear that if there was anything he could do to help, all I needed to do was ask.

I walked away truly moved by the true compassion and concern that he and all of the parents had shown for both my daughter and me. The love and care that I experienced from those kind souls still gives me faith in people today.

I was so touched that I had to call Anne and share it with her. She was in the car on her way to the fields and was delighted to hear that everyone had been so positive and receptive. Anne was not terribly surprised though, as she had shared Katie's situation with folks before. In those instances, she had also been happily surprised by how often others had been touched by mental illness in one way or another.

A while later, once Anne had come up and joined me on the sidelines, Katie was up at bat, and her team was losing. Anne and I sat tensely in our lawn chairs, a little worried that the pressure of being behind by a couple of runs at the bottom of the last inning would make it difficult for Katie to perform to her best abilities. But she ended up crushing the ball all the way across to the edge of the outfield, bringing three runners in and winning the game.

"I may have to put you on my older kids' team," said the coach affectionately as he hugged her with pride. It was clear that the knowledge of Katie's mental health issues didn't affect the way he looked at her at all, and that brought me an immense amount of peace.

Though it was difficult raising a child with mental illness, along with two others, something about having the support of those around us made it just a little easier. Though I was still a little hesitant to be totally open about Katie's condition after this instance, I certainly felt more comfortable and optimistic about sharing our family's difficulties. I knew the stigma persisted, but I also knew that people could be exceedingly kind and understanding, and for my little girl, that's what I had to hope for.

MOM

Spring 2008

Katie is about the strongest person I know. No, not "about"—
she *is* the strongest person I know!

Each year, the students in sixth grade get to go on a weeklong
camping trip to explore nature—and Katie was in sixth grade. It
can be difficult to be away from home for that long, especially if
you haven't been gone for so long before. So, Katie was very anxious about being away from us for such a lengthy period of time. I
completely understood; I know that the first time I was away from
home for more than a few days, I became very homesick.

Despite her misgivings, she wanted to go and have the same
experience that everyone else was having. We had talked with her
counselor and school nurse prior to the trip so everyone would
know that Katie might struggle while she was there. We made
sure Katie would be able to call home if need be.

It would have been easy for Katie to say, "No, I don't want to
go," and we wouldn't have made her. But this kid, with such courage and strength, wanted to try to make it through the week. And

you know what? She did just that! Was it easy? Absolutely not. She struggled just to get on the bus to leave for camp. But she went, she participated, and at the end of the week, she came back home!

Rob and I already knew Katie was capable of anything she set her mind to. But once Katie was able to overcome her anxiety and be a normal kid at sixth grade camp, we were hopeful that she could understand that about herself too.

This triumph did seem to give her more confidence in some ways. Nonetheless, Katie continued to overlook her value and worth for many years afterward—something that wouldn't be fully uncovered until she was almost twenty-two years old.

LAUREN

Being the proud person that I am, it's difficult for me to admit it, but I've never coped very effectively with Katie's mental health challenges. I tend to bottle all my emotions up, determined to be strong for my family and for myself.

When Katie first started having problems, I simply escaped into my *Harry Potter* books instead of facing my emotions head on. Harry, Ron, and Hermione became my best friends, and I sought solace in their lives, aching to be in a world that wasn't my own. I found comfort in the familiar words on the pages; I knew that no matter how many times I read each *Harry Potter* book, the words and the feelings they evoked would be the same. With all my routines ravaged by Katie's wildly spinning emotional state, I clung to that stability.

As I entered middle school, I also became very interested in music. Broadening my taste, I was able to discover sounds that were so complex and full and beautiful that they would make my heart strain, desperate to capture the music and make it a part of me. It was impossible not to be moved by the story that could be told by the mingling of instruments and the emotion that could be conveyed with a few vivid lyrics. To avoid the harshness of Katie's declining mental health, I would sink into my music, closing my ears to the sobbing in the room next to mine. Often, I would sing, trying to expel my suppressed emotions through my vocal cords. This was quite cathartic, but it didn't get at the root of my pain.

In middle school and early high school, I largely turned away from my family and the darkness that held it in its clutches. Instead, I focused more on my social status and friendships. Young and distracted by the desire to be cool, I made many friends, but I often lied or embellished other aspects of my life to fit in.

At this point, I didn't talk a lot about Katie anymore because I didn't know how people would react, and I wasn't really sure how to explain anyway. But I did pretend that I had visited places I'd never seen, kissed boys who didn't exist, and broken rules that I never would've dared break. I had been such a sweet, unassuming kid my entire life, but at that point, my personality clearly shifted significantly.

Sometimes I wonder if I acted like such a brat as a teenager because I wanted so badly to be normal in some way. Everything going on at home was so far from normal that I did whatever I could to be a regular kid when I was away from there. Unfortunately, a lot of the lengths I went to in an effort to be "normal" were hurtful to me and those around me. So, though I did turn to my friends as a means of coping, it wasn't a positive situation.

Then, when I was in the ninth grade, I went through a depression. Though I was still a nice person—at my core, the same person I'd always been—the poor choices I'd made in my interactions with my friends rendered me virtually friendless. With each passing month, a different friend was leaving me in the dust, pushing me into a rapid downward spiral. For the first time in my life, I thought I could kind of understand how Katie felt sometimes.

When I turned back to my parents, seeking comfort and encouragement, I was sorely disappointed by the response I received. They were sympathetic the first one, two, or three times I came to them, overwhelmed with sadness and anxiety. But after a while, my dad said something along the lines of, "You've already told us this before," when I described my feelings.

I guess my parents didn't understand that I, the child who was always okay, was truly *not* okay. I needed the kind of support they normally provided to Katie. But in their eyes, I was just being dramatic. They wouldn't realize the depth of the depression I was facing until I talked to them about it again much later as an adult. But at the time, I felt completely closed off from everyone, entirely deprived of compassion or understanding.

With all this lonely pain on my shoulders, I barely took the time to commend Katie on triumphs like making it through sixth grade camp or muddling through the seventh grade. I felt like I wasn't really close to anyone, and my support system had crumbled into nothing. It would take a long time to build it back up again.

DAD

Fall 2008

As I mentioned earlier, I've always been a strict disciplinarian, and I didn't have any qualms about yelling at my kids when they were acting up or even using corporal punishment if necessary. I wanted my parenting to be consistent with all my children, and when I said I would do something—such as punish them if they took a particular action—I followed through without fail.

Over time though, I found that my approach to dealing with Katie was counterproductive. When I raised my voice, it was far more likely to make things worse rather than better. It wasn't easy for me to accept this and change, but accept it and change I did . . . eventually. I knew it was critical for me to shift my parenting strategy to be able to effectively deal with Katie and her mental illness.

I still remember quite clearly when I came to that realization. Katie played softball on a select team, and we all enjoyed watching her play and cheering her on.

One day, when we were at the ballpark, Katie was hit by a ball while at the plate. If I remember correctly, the pitch nicked her thumb or her pinky. It really didn't seem like that big of a deal to me, but as Anne, Katie, and I were walking through the park after the game, Katie continued to carry on about her finger hurting. I thought, *This is part of playing softball, so suck it up!* Eventually, I barked at her to knock it off and toughen up. It worked like a charm—assuming I was wanting her to go into a full-blown meltdown.

I can still recall that look on Anne's face as she glared at me. Any husband out there knows the look I'm talking about. It's the one that says, *You are a complete idiot . . . How could you have been so stupid as to think that was a good call?* It's the one that says, *You, and you alone, are responsible for this.*

I realized then and there that my way of dealing with things was no longer going to work, and I had to make a concerted effort to reevaluate my approach. The problem was that I didn't have another bag of tricks—I had exhausted my tools in childrearing and didn't know what to do. As a result, I found myself backing off and doing nothing—all the way through Katie's adolescent years.

Now, to be clear, none of our kids ever had serious behavioral problems, so it's not like I was letting Katie run amok. It was just that we tended to protect her from the consequences of her actions.

For instance, although Katie's behavior drastically improved after we learned of her diagnosis and focused on ways to treat her mental illness, she would still occasionally act out. It's possible the fact that we often prioritized her in an effort to care for her mental state caused her to demand additional attention when she was doing just fine. Or perhaps this was just the typical behavior of a child—they're not going to be perfect all the time. Regardless, when Katie behaved in a way I would have deemed unacceptable for one reason or another, I didn't quite know how to handle it. So, I wouldn't address it at all—I'd just retreat. That generally made Anne happy because Katie wouldn't escalate.

Another example of this was how we sheltered her from many school responsibilities and deadlines. These were protected by federal law and her 504 plan—something offered to students who do fine academically but require certain accommodations. Because of this, Katie was afforded more time to take a test, or even given the option to take a test in a separate room, and was allowed to get up and walk around in the hallway when anxious. She needed these accommodations to get the most out of her schooling, but they did perhaps give her an inaccurate sense of what the "real world" would be like. The real world where you're still expected to do your work, do it well, and do it on time—regardless of mental illness.

It was nothing serious, but over time, I realized that we were protecting Katie from the growth that we gain from dealing with consequences. I ended up having to start imposing those types of repercussions, saying "no" when it was warranted, in different little ways, which ended up creating a rift in my relationship with Katie.

Ultimately, this also impacted the way in which I dealt with my other two daughters. Again, it wasn't like I let them get away with whatever they wanted. But since I was going so easy on Katie, I felt constrained from dealing with the other two girls in the fashion that I thought best.

Thankfully, they are really great kids, so going easy on them hasn't seemed to do them any harm. Anne and I are extremely lucky that all of our children are intelligent, capable, and motivated to contribute meaningfully to society—with or without mental illness.

MOM

It's really important that both parents communicate frequently and effectively and be on the same page with discipline. But that's not always easy to do. I think that when you have a child with a mental illness, you sometimes have to change how you parent them, including how you enforce rules.

In our family, Rob was always more the disciplinarian, and it was *I have these rules, and you're going to follow them and do what I say, or you're going to be in trouble.* However, we realized that when we tried to discipline Katie in particular, we would all end up yelling back and forth, and it would just become chaotic. So, I learned that when Katie was escalating, I just needed to be on an even keel to help her calm down.

That's something that Rob had to learn too, and it was hard for him because that wasn't how he operated. But he knew that was the change he was going to have to make in order to be effective with Katie.

This was crucial because Katie was the one who we usually needed to discipline. See, Lauren was always good and followed the rules, whereas Katie would just push every limit. In fact, typically, if Lauren was in trouble, it was because she and Katie were fighting—and a lot of that happened because Katie always instigated things. (Of course, Sarah would require discipline too eventually, but since she's five years younger than Katie, we didn't have to worry about that for a little while.)

So, learning how to effectively discipline Katie was super important, especially as she got older and her behavior issues changed from hitting her sister or arguing to *I'm cutting and I'm sad and I'm going to take a handful of pills*. Though it took us some getting used to, this method of dealing with Katie helped us enforce rules without sending her totally off the deep end, even when she was having a hard time with her mental health.

LAUREN

Summary 2009

As Katie grew older, she (mostly) learned how to ignore the shadows inside her head. They were always circling, biding their time, preparing to pounce, but she was usually able to keep them at bay. This allowed her to come into herself more and grow into her true personality. Though she had been a mischievous little rascal as a child, by the time she was twelve, she'd developed into a selfless, compassionate individual who loved unconditionally.

If I was having a bad day, she would offer me a hug. She sometimes wrote my parents little notes, thanking them for everything they had done for her. She put her whole heart into each of her friendships, even when her friends looked down on her for struggling with her mental health. She encouraged my whole family to get more involved in church, even though it sometimes seems that God has cursed her with these mental health challenges.

Fortunately, at this point in her journey, Katie was on her way to establishing a new normal for herself. She was learning to

manage her illness, and her life was starting to get back on track
... at least for a while.

You are not your illness.
You have an individual
story to tell. You have a
name, a history, a personality. Staying yourself is
part of the battle.

—*Julian Seifter*

PART 3

LAUREN

Fall 2009

When Katie was in the eighth grade, she started to experience something new—something somehow scarier than
anything we had encountered before.

She began to hear things.

At the time, Katie thought she was hallucinating. However,
we soon realized she was actually being visited by intrusive
thoughts—deafening, dark, obsessive. Now, her mental illness
presented itself through vivid mental pictures of Katie self-harming and the little voice inside her head urging her to kill herself.

There was one recurring picture that Katie simply could not
shake: she was in our backyard, hanging from the tree farthest
away from the house, the yellow rope from our garage wound
tightly around her neck. The imagery that plagued her for so long
still haunts me because I can envision that exact scene. I have no
doubt that it sometimes haunts her too.

Despite my parents' best efforts, they ended up not trusting their ability to keep Katie safe. After all, they couldn't have eyes on her every second of every day. And the fact that the resources for Katie's vision of suicide were readily available was certainly unnerving. They had to do something to prevent that horrific imagery from becoming reality—even if that meant doing something they had avoided for so long.

For the first time, Katie was hospitalized.

SARAH

Fall 2009

I was watching TV with Mom in the family room when Katie suddenly burst in, looking panicked.

"Mom, I need to talk to you." She sounded upset. I wasn't really sure what was going on, but I was a curious eight-year-old kid, so I remained seated on the couch, watching everything. "Um, Sarah, can you please leave?" Katie said uncomfortably after a moment.

Darn it. "Okay."

I got up and walked around the loveseat, heading into the hallway. Then, though I pretended to go to my room, I hung back and listened to everything Katie said.

"Mom, I keep hearing a voice in my head," Katie muttered, just loud enough for me to hear from my spot outside the family room. "It keeps telling me to go outside and hang myself on the tree in the backyard."

Mom responded, but I was too preoccupied with what I'd just heard to pay attention. Was Katie doing badly again?

I snapped myself out of it as I heard Katie's voice once more. "For a while, I told the voice that I couldn't do that because I didn't want to. Then, I decided I *did* want to do it, but I told the voice that there was no way for me to do it. And then . . . the voice said there was stuff in the garage I could use . . . and . . . I just got really freaked out."

As Katie started crying, I ran back to my room, feeling rattled. I still wasn't really sure what was going on, but it clearly wasn't anything good.

The next day, I went to the counselor at school and told her everything that had happened. I was afraid to tell Mom I'd heard Katie's tearful confession because I thought she was going to be angry with me for eavesdropping. But the counselor wisely told me I should talk to my mom about it 'cause it was important for her to know what I'd heard.

That night, when I got home from school, I admitted everything to Mom and told her how worried I was. To my relief, she assured me that everything was going be okay and that Katie's medicine had just reacted badly. At that point, I believed the doctors just needed to work on fixing that minor issue, and then Katie would be better. I had a positive attitude about the situation, but it didn't end up being as easy as I'd thought. As it turned out, we had a long, hard road ahead of us.

LAUREN

Fall 2009

It was Thanksgiving Day five years after Katie was diagnosed. The whole family had gathered at our grandparents' house in celebration of the holiday, and everyone was bustling around the kitchen and dining room, eagerly awaiting the feast of turkey and stuffing. Everyone but Katie.

I located her in the living room. She was sitting rigidly in a chair, her hands clutching at the edge of the white seat cushion, her eyes wide and mouth twitching as if she were talking to an invisible person. Approaching her cautiously, I laid a gentle hand on her shoulder. I'm not exactly sure what happened—perhaps I scared her—but all of a sudden, she was out of her seat and lying on the carpet. She didn't even bother to right herself but continued to loll on her side.

"Please go away," muttered Katie in a low, quiet voice that nevertheless conveyed her utter terror and confusion. "Get out, get out."

"Me?" I whispered, pointing uncertainly to myself. *I just got here. What could I have done wrong already?*

She whimpered, curling up into a ball and desperately clutching her hands over her ears. Brow crinkling, chin scrunching, she began to cry, terrified sobs racking through her body with enough force to cause her limbs to shake. I stared helplessly as she rocked back and forth on the ground, moaning and mumbling to herself. I had never thought of her as crazy, but in that moment, she looked truly insane.

"Leave me alone," she groaned, and I realized with sudden, horrible clarity what was happening. Katie was covering her ears to block out the sounds of people who didn't exist and squinting her eyes shut against images that weren't even real. Deep in the recesses of her mind, voices were speaking to her, commanding her to hurt herself. I'd never seen anyone more petrified in my whole life, and the fact that she herself was the source of her fear made the situation a thousand times worse.

"Katie—" I tried to console her as I reached a hand toward her shivering arm.

"Don't touch me!" she suddenly shrieked, her eyes snapping open. "Get away from me," she sobbed. "I don't want to hurt you."

"Okay," I whispered, not wanting to leave her side but understanding her need for space. Moments later, my mom rushed into the room. I hung back, too much in shock to be of any use as she knelt next to Katie, murmuring soothingly.

At that moment, as a sixteen-year-old girl, I gained a true understanding of fear and the sheer helplessness that comes along with it. Eventually, I would become so familiar with the fear that I would become almost desensitized to it, too accustomed to Katie's raging emotions and associated behavior to react strongly. But at the time, I was completely thrown by what was then uncharacteristic behavior, and the terror I experienced made that memory stick out as one of the worst.

LAUREN

Fall 2009

Katie wasn't okay.

The thought of her trembling face haunted me, following me from class to dinner to bed. Fear, anxiety, uncertainty, and helplessness welled up in me until the flooding emotions rendered me mute.

I had no outlet. My parents were busy taking Katie on walks and drives, holding her close as she sobbed uncontrollably, all the while whispering hopelessly to each other. My youngest sister, Sarah, was eight, so she was old enough to notice what was going on this time, but I couldn't cry to her. I needed to be strong for her. I couldn't even talk to my friends; I was afraid that they would look at Katie differently—look at *me* differently.

One day, I couldn't contain the rampaging emotions anymore. Katie had been getting worse and worse, and I knew my parents were thinking about taking her to the hospital, even though she begged them not to.

I splintered.

"What's the matter?" asked my friend Alexis. Her straight bru-nette hair brushed the worn rectangular lunch table as she leaned forward to cup my arm. "You look like you're about to cry."

"I'm fine." My voice cracked on the giant lump in my throat. Tears were forming before I could stop them. I wasn't fooling any-body.

"Oh no, Lauren—don't cry! Tell us what's wrong," coaxed Steffi, her concerned brown eyes peeping at me from under her dark bangs.

Hallie, Kensi, and Jenny also offered words of encouragement and invitation. Kyra, whom I didn't get along with, just sat silently in her spot, her arms folded. These were my closest friends in high school, and as their kindness and concern washed over me, I broke down.

"It's my sister," I sobbed, my face crinkling up in misery as I looked down at the table.

"Katie or Sarah?" frowned Alexis.

"Katie. She's—she's in trouble."

"What do you mean?" prompted Hallie, her piercing blue eyes serious as they caught mine.

"Look, guys, there are some things that have been going on in my family that I haven't told you about." I hesitated.

"Is that why you've been so quiet and distracted lately?" asked Alexis, squeezing my arm.

I nodded. "It's been awful. She keeps seeing things and hearing things telling her to hurt herself. She's been biting and scratching and choking herself again, and my parents keep having to hide the knives because she's always trying to find them. They're afraid to even take her to school. I think they're gonna take her to the hos-pital." I mopped at my sopping eyes with the sleeve of my shirt. "I'm scared."

One by one, my friends got up and crowded around me in a big hug while I remained collapsed in my chair, my shoulders shak-ing. I barely glanced up when Kyra, the only one who showed little interest or concern about my emotional state, got up and marched across the cafeteria.

By the time the bell rang, signaling the end of lunch, my face was still glazed with tears, but I was managing a small smile. I felt a little bit better knowing that I did have a support system. I just had to learn to be more trusting and forthcoming.

Unfortunately, my small moment of relief didn't last long. At the end of the day, Kensi caught up with me by my locker in the sophomore bay.

"Lauren, I have something to talk to you about. I've been feeling really conflicted over this because I know that telling you about it is going to make you angry and upset, and you know I don't like drama, but I think it's only fair that you know."

I looked at her, anxiety clawing at my chest.

"Kyra's been talking about you," she explained gently. "About your sister actually. I guess that the second she heard what you said at lunch, she went and told the next person she could find."

"What'd they say?" I gasped, hands covering my mouth.

"Apparently whoever she told was really nice about it. They were like, 'Wow, that's really horrible. I feel awful for her family.' But Kyra didn't like that response. She said, 'No, that's crazy. That girl is insane.'" Kensi hesitated. "She's been talking about it to other people too, saying some pretty hateful things. She even wondered . . . well, if you could have some crazy in you too. If it runs in your family."

I didn't respond. Blood rushed angrily to my head as my cheeks grew hot. My palms and feet went numb. I hardly knew where I was, I was so infuriated.

"Lauren, I know you're upset, but please don't start anything," pleaded Kensi, her long, golden hair swinging as she pulled on my arm. I hadn't even realized I'd turned away, fists clenched, intent upon finding Kyra.

"Me?" I shrieked, as Kensi flapped her hands at me, trying to quiet me down. "I never start anything with her. She picks on me and picks on me and picks on me, and I never stand up for myself because I don't want to deal with the drama. I'm the bigger person every single time, but this time . . . That's my *sister*, my little sister . . ." I lost all coherence as my voice wound down to a low groan, and I dissolved into tears on the red tile floor.

LAUREN

Fall 2009

The house was eerily quiet. Mom and Dad looked at each other a lot as they wandered around, trying to look busy and normal, but they didn't say much. Even Sarah was at a loss for words, and she usually liked to talk just to hear her own voice. I felt like I would never speak again.

The picture on the box was of kittens and yellow flowers. This bright image was completely at odds with my mood. My knees pressed into the carpet as I leaned forward, trying to concentrate through the haze of grief overwhelming my mind. The puzzle piece in my shaking hand almost fit into the open space but not quite. I set it back down uninterestedly, barely noticing as another tear slipped past my heavy eyelids.

Katie's keening sobs echoed in my ears even though she'd been gone for almost twenty-four hours. She had pleaded with my parents, beseeching them to let her stay. She hadn't wanted to go to the hospital.

She'd had to go.

I had hardly eaten or slept or even moved since my parents had taken her. I knew that she needed serious and immediate help that she could only get through inpatient, but the devastated look on my sister's face as she was led to the car haunted me. It was all I could think about.

In a halfhearted effort to distract myself, I had pulled a puzzle out of the large wooden cabinet that had once supported a salt-water fish tank. Listless and dull, I'd sunk onto the carpet in the family room and gotten to work. It was somewhat helpful. At least I had something undemanding to occupy my time while I processed my sadness and fear. Still, my thoughts were quick and impatient; my mind would settle on one thing and immediately switch to another, then another. I felt hyperaware of everything to the point that my skin almost hurt. I was restless but too emotionally exhausted to even get up.

My parents had allowed me to stay home from school. It wasn't even discussed. All day, I sat on the floor and tested out puzzle pieces. I took my time. It was a large puzzle, but I made little progress with each hour that passed. I felt like I didn't care about anything. The truth is that I cared too much.

By the second day of Katie's stay in the hospital, I had recovered enough to hang on to a few of my fleeting thoughts.

Why, God? How could you do this to my little sister? To my family? We haven't done anything terribly wrong. I sniffled. *How could you let something like mental illness exist in this world?*

I felt like raging and screaming and shaking my fist up at God. I had never felt so angry in my life. However, my fury with God was eclipsed by my guilt for thinking badly of Him. Confused, I turned away from God entirely, not willing to let Him off the hook but not willing to express my anger at Him either.

Katie returned home after three days. My emotions had flared up so intensely that they had burnt themselves out. Apathy and numbness had settled in again. I hardly glanced up as she walked in the door with Mom.

The puzzle piece held between my fingers slid into the open space.

LAUREN

Fall 2009

Sometimes, I would open up about my sister's condition and the way it affected me. I'd hesitantly share my heartbreak, my fear, and my loneliness with my aunt or my grandmother or my papa. Unfortunately, each time I thought that sharing my emotions would make me feel better, I found I was sorely mistaken.

"But think about your parents," they'd say. "How hard it must be for them to have a daughter with mental illness. Think about Sarah. She has to watch her older sister have emotional breakdowns all the time. Think about Katie. She's the one actually suffering because of her mental illness."

You're right, I always thought bitterly to myself. *Why should I be so upset? It's obviously so much harder on everyone else. Silly me.*

Then, I'd resolve never to speak of it again. And I wouldn't . . . until the pain became too unbearable, and I couldn't carry the burden on my own anymore.

SARAH

Fall 2009

When I was in the third grade, the first time stuff was going on with Katie that I can actually remember, I had a few different coping mechanisms I would use. Aunt Molly and Uncle Jim always let me go over to their house and just get away from it all. I didn't necessarily have to talk about things if I didn't want to, but they always offered me the option and let me spend the night. Or I would go to dinner with them or Aunt Maggie. It was always nice to have that support from my extended family, and I appreciated them being willing to set aside time and attention for me.

I also talked to Miss Singer a couple of times a week. She was my elementary school counselor. I remember I was scared to talk to her at first because I'd only known Miss C, the previous counselor. But once I talked to Miss Singer, I became really close with her, and she helped me cope with everything. In fact, she continued to be there for me even after I graduated from elementary school and moved on to middle and high school.

Along with those coping mechanisms, I would try reaching out to my friends for support.

At the beginning, I was a little nervous to open up to people about Katie. I actually remember Mom telling me I shouldn't necessarily talk to my friends about Katie's mental illness because it could scare them. She worried that if they told their parents, they might not want their kids to come over anymore. Basically, though she knew Katie would never hurt anyone or pose a threat, she was concerned that knowledge of Katie's mental illness could mess up my friendships.

I didn't listen. I told my two best friends what was going on, and I'm pretty sure they told their parents, but it didn't change anything about our friendships. And after my friends were supportive, I was more comfortable talking about it.

One of the two friends I told initially was Aubrey, and she became the main person I would confide in about my troubles at home. I talked to her every day after school on the bus ride home because, at this point, things were hard pretty much on a daily basis. So, every afternoon on the bus, I would talk to her about what had happened the night before. Aubrey has a brother who deals with the same thing, so she was able to understand. When I would confide in Aubrey about my family's problems and hear about hers, that support and true understanding of how mental illness can affect a person was really valuable to me.

Looking back across my whole life, I feel like there are plenty of people who understand it because it affects a lot of individuals. So, when I talk about it even today, whoever I'm talking to can usually relate somehow. That brings me a lot of comfort and makes me feel like I'm not totally alone in my situation. And it lets me show people that they're not alone in their situation either.

As far as dealing with Katie's mental health struggles, when things were bad, there wasn't really an in between for me. I either really wanted to get out of the house and be with my friends, where I could talk about what was going on and generally make myself busy so I didn't have to think about it. Or I wanted to just be home and be sad about it. Basically, I would go out and not come home for a long time or I just wouldn't want to do anything at all. Either way, I was pretty reliant on my friends to help me deal with what was going on a lot of the time.

MOM

Winter 2009

As Katie continued to struggle with her mental health, she was in and out of IOP. The problem with that was there were so many different people dealing with her, and the various doctors had differing opinions on what was wrong. I've gotta say . . . It's pretty difficult to find an effective treatment when there isn't even agreement on the diagnosis.

One of the times Katie was in IOP, there was another doctor, Dr. Salsburg, who saw her. Much to our surprise, Dr. Salsburg told us that Katie had obsessive-compulsive disorder (OCD).

"What?" we asked, astonished. "There's no way. Why do you think that?"

"Well, she prays a lot."

That just seemed nuts to us. At the time, Rob and I thought OCD was *you wash your hands a lot, you count, you double-check all the locks, you have these repetitive things that go on and on.* And I'm sorry, praying a lot? That repetition doesn't make you

OCD—it makes you, I don't know, a good Christian? It seemed crazy to me.

Despite our misgivings, Katie was put on OCD medicine. However, it ended up making things worse, so we took her off that and didn't do anything more for it at that point. We just didn't feel she needed treatment for OCD based on Dr. Salsburg's reasoning at the time.

Unfortunately, if that doctor could have meaningfully articulated why she felt Katie had OCD, we would have gotten on the right path a lot sooner. As it turns out, Katie *does* have OCD. If we had been given an appropriate explanation for such a diagnosis, we probably would have been able to help Katie with some of her other symptoms a lot earlier. But at the time, we were totally clueless. As far as we knew, that doctor had no idea what she was talking about.

Now, looking back, it seems obvious that Katie always had OCD. From the beginning of her journey with mental illness, she dealt with obsessive, unwanted, unwelcome thoughts that were in her head, and that's a huge part of what OCD is (or, at least, how it affects her). For example, her imaginary friends who constantly told her to hurt herself were probably manifestations of her OCD. Sadly, at the time, we just hadn't understood that.

LAUREN

My mom is the most incredible woman. As hard as Katie's mental illness is on Katie herself, it's also crushingly difficult for my mom. After all, she has to watch her child, her little girl, struggle constantly with her sense of worth. And as strong as my mom is, she's also sensitive. So, everything was really tough on her—more so than it was for my father.

As amazing and inspiring as my mother is, she's not perfect. And one thing that I struggled with a lot growing up was my mom's decidedly placating nature. Now, in general, this was not an issue. I mean, my mom is just a naturally sweet woman who would prefer to avoid all conflict. As someone who also dislikes conflict, I identified with and appreciated that. But there were definite drawbacks to this quality of hers.

It was a Saturday morning, and I was watching one of my shows on TV. Still wearing my pajamas, my hair a sloppy mess, I was slouched on the couch, still kind of waking up.

Perhaps roused by the gentle hum of the television, Katie plodded in not long later, rubbing her eyes and stretching. Acting the typical teenager, I ignored her completely, pretending not to have seen her. I continued to lie there as though catatonic, hoping to avoid conversation so early in the morning.

"What are you watching?"

Ugh. "It's a crime show."

"Oh." For a moment, she was quiet, standing still between the kitchen and the living room. Then . . . "Well, I want to watch something else."

"Katie, I was in here first. I'm already in the middle of watching this show. You have to wait."

"No, we both need to agree on something. And I don't like this."

"Katie . . ."

"I said I don't like it!"

"Well, I don't really care."

"You're being such a bitch!" Katie exploded.

Her irrational fury was so hot and bright that it summoned my mom, who had been in the basement doing laundry. "What's going on?" she demanded, breathing a little bit heavily from charging up the stairs.

"I was—"

"Lauren won't compromise on what show we watch!"

"M—"

"She always has to have everything her way. I'm really freaking sick of it."

"Well, she called me a bitch—"

"All right, that's enough." My mom turned to Katie. "How about . . . Why don't you get dressed, and we can go on a drive. Maybe we can go by McDonald's or somewhere for lunch."

My jaw dropped. "But Mom!"

"Cool it. I do not want to deal with you two fighting. You get to watch what you want to watch. That's the end of it."

I stared, hurt, as they disappeared to the back of the house to get changed. I hadn't even had a chance to tell my side of the story. So, I looked like a big jerk, while Katie was being rewarded with lunch out even though she had called me a bitch. How was that fair?

This sort of thing happened constantly as I was growing up. I liked to think of it as my mom taking the easy way out. Made vulnerable by her fragile mental health, Katie was extremely difficult to console. When she was highly emotional, whether angry or sad, it took a lot of time and effort to help her find equilibrium again. On the other hand, I didn't put up too much of a fuss, often just sinking into a silent simmer. So, eager to avoid raging emotions, my mom would favor Katie over me, not because she loved me any less but simply because she wanted everything to be okay.

The thing is I wasn't okay. I may not have been as vocal about it, but I still had feelings. I hated for them to be brushed aside. And this may have been what incited me to start brushing aside my feelings myself. Maybe that contributed to me later thinking my problems and emotions didn't matter as much.

Unfortunately, my mom would have to deal with the ongoing repercussions of continuously "taking the easy way out" with Katie. Her habit of appeasing Katie fostered a sense of entitlement in my sister, causing her to expect to have her way, no matter the circumstances.

In essence, Katie has an unrealistic sense of how people should treat her. In the real world, no one is going to validate her every thought and feeling. People aren't going to accommodate her every wish and desire. They aren't going to sacrifice their own plans and goals in favor of Katie's. But since that's how my mom has always treated Katie, that's what Katie expects of everyone.

This attitude often strains our relationship, as she doesn't understand why I won't bend over backwards for her. For instance, it seems that in her mind, if she wants to spend a certain amount of time with me, I should want to spend that time with her. It doesn't matter to her that I have my own family and friends and ample responsibilities to juggle. It doesn't even matter to her that I may not want to hang out with her if she's recently been unkind to me. From her perspective, if she wants something, I should give it to her. That's how it's always been, so that's how it should always be.

This is an ongoing challenge for my parents too. Now that Katie's life is on a great trajectory, my mom is attempting to establish boundaries and break the codependency that has always characterized their relationship. However, it's extremely difficult to shift the dynamics after years and years of consistently giving in to and appeasing Katie.

What can you learn from this? Don't rely on taking the easy way out every time. Of course, that's much easier said than done. When you're worried that your loved one will harm themselves if you don't give them their way, of course, you're going to do whatever you can to placate them. But be very mindful of how often you're doing this. You may just find that you've created an endless problem that will color your relationship with your loved one for many years to come.

I love my mom with everything in me. I can't imagine doing a better job raising a family with mental illness thrown into the mix. I can't even imagine doing half as good of a job! And just knowing her sweet and loving nature, it's hard for me to hold it against her too much, especially because I know that she only has the best of intentions. Nonetheless, this treatment seriously affected me as an adolescent, and it still affects me today.

LAUREN

Winter 2010

K atie was all right, but she wasn't really better. She was no longer losing herself to the harmful thoughts and images tres-
passing in her mind. She had returned to school and turned herself
to the daunting task of catching up with her work. Every day, she
took her medicine and went about her routine. But the darkness
continued to simmer inside of her. It hadn't quite abated yet.

For eight months, Katie hung on by a thread. Our family
pointedly ignored the fact that she was bound to fall straight into
the darkness again—soon. We pretended (or perhaps just hoped)
that true improvement was gradually coming along.

It wasn't.

LAUREN

Spring 2010

"**S**hut up!" bellowed Katie, cheeks red and eyes crazed.

I didn't even deign to answer—simply rolled my eyes and tossed my long hair. I'd finally emerged from my bedroom after a long afternoon of basking in the misery of my teenage angst. Katie had tried to talk to me, but I'd made some wise-crack response, and the argument had escalated from there.

Like many teenagers, when I turned sixteen, my personality took a sharp downhill turn. I was sarcastic, condescending, and generally rude when I was at home. My family didn't take well to my suddenly acerbic personality. Katie, who is particularly sensitive, struggled perhaps the most with my abrasive behavior.

After every dramatic encounter with her, I would trudge around outside or hole myself up in my room, swallowed up by guilt and shame. Even still, I get a sick feeling when I think of how harsh and rude I was to her and the rest of my family during that stage of my life.

"You're the worst sister ever!" Katie spat, jumping to her feet. Her whole face glowed with anger.

My mouth dropped open, and I stood as well. "Are you kidding me? After all you put me through? After all you put our family through? I've tried so hard to be a good sister to you, but you never appreciate it."

For a moment, Katie seemed so offended that she was at a loss for words. However, it wasn't long before she regained her voice. "All I've put you through? What do you want me to do, just get it over with quick? If I kill myself now, you guys can be sad, but you won't have to deal with me anymore."

"You know that's not what I meant . . ."

"But you probably wouldn't care anyway. You don't care about anyone except yourself. That's why no one can stand you. You don't have any friends, and no one in the family wants to be around you either. You fuck up everything, no matter what you do. I wish I didn't even have you as a sister." Katie breathed harshly, her chest heaving, after her heated speech. Refusing to cry, I watched her for a moment, my hands balled into fists.

That was one of the hardest parts of growing up with Katie when she was under the influence, to any extent, of her mental illness. She could say the most hateful, heart-wrenching things. She could make the one comment that she knew would hit me the hardest and chase away sleep for many nights to come. She knew me better than almost anyone, so she knew how to make me hurt—and she never failed to do just that.

The worst part was that Katie could say these things . . . and nothing would happen. It wasn't her fault, after all. It was her mental illness. She didn't mean it, and she never would have said it if she were herself.

But she did say it. And I heard it, and I felt the pain of it. Regardless of how sorry she was afterward, her words affected me deeply. They cracked my self-esteem and pummeled my relationship with her until we could barely stand to be in the same room with each other.

The biggest challenge for me was learning how to respond to the hateful comments Katie made when lost in the throes of her mental illness. Though I'd been timid and shy as a child, I became increasingly strong-willed and opinionated as I got older. If I thought something, I was sure to say it, and I rarely had the self-control to refrain from sharing my opinions around my sensitive sister.

Whenever she bowled me over with her caustic comments, I was sure to retaliate, too angry and upset to care about her delicate state. By this point, I wanted to stick up for myself, and I was tired of walking on eggshells. Unfortunately, while Katie had an excuse for her words and behavior, I did not. And though some of the points I made were fair, a lot of times, I simply perpetuated the stigma associated with mental illness, something I reflect on with regret and remorse today.

"Whatever, psycho. At least I can take care of myself. I don't require everyone's attention 24-7. Sometimes I don't even think you're trying to fight it."

Katie's eyes got bright, and she lunged for the kitchen shears that were sitting haphazardly on the coffee table. There was already plenty of space between us, but I took a startled step backward, alarmed that she suddenly had a weapon. I watched warily, ready to jump out of the way if she moved in my direction (though she had never been violent toward me before). Her teeth were gritted, and her eyes were moving from side to side, almost as if she couldn't even see me anymore.

A second later, she hurled the shears at the couch. They bounced off the cushion, glanced off the coffee table, and thudded on the floor as she whirled around and stalked out of the house, the front door slamming behind her. I sank into the armchair, my extremities weak and my heart beating rapidly.

She had seriously considered stabbing me. I saw the shadow in her eyes telling me I was about to bleed. But then I saw her fight it. I saw her use all the strength she could scrounge up to get the shears away from her and get as far away from me as possible.

But she wasn't just trying to get away because I had hurt her; she was trying to get away so that she wouldn't hurt me. She wanted to protect me.

To this day, Katie has never hurt anyone. She may experience murderous rage from time to time, but she always puts everyone's well-being first. Her mental illness tries to divert her loving heart, but she is simply too good of a person to ever intentionally hurt someone, mental illness or not.

I stared at the shears laying forlornly on the ground as my mom and dad, who had just emerged from the back of the house, scrambled out the door, calling Katie's name. After a minute or so, I calmly stood up and walked back to my room, letting my door slam behind me in true teenage fashion.

DAD

Each child is different, and even the reason or motivation for their conduct can be misunderstood. For instance, when Lauren and Katie were little, it appeared Katie was much more like me and Lauren was more like her mother. I say "appeared," as that turned out not to be the case at all.

As a child, I was often referred to as "strong-willed" or just outright "bad." I don't recall it, but apparently, my kindergarten teacher got frustrated with me one day and told me in front of the class that I was bad and would grow up to be put in prison.

However, my great-grandmother, who was a teacher, was fond of saying, "Give me a strong-willed child any day—they may be difficult to get on the right path, but once on, they will never falter." Anyway, because of my own personality as a child, Anne and I just thought Katie's behavior was her being strong-willed.

Lauren, on the other hand, was always trying to be the peace-maker by routinely giving in to her sister. Because of this, I often worried about my oldest child not being strong enough to stand up for herself. Were you to meet Lauren today, you would laugh at the very notion, but at the time, it was a concern of mine.

One thing I witnessed as a result of what our family went through was the transformation that Lauren underwent through the periods of Katie's illness. I believe that everyone in a family tends to have a particular role. For example, my older brother is the one who sets the example and does everything right, while I . . . Well, let's just say I'm not my brother and leave it at that.

In our young family, Lauren saw herself as the kind, sweet child—what some might call the "good child." Lauren never got in trouble at home or at school. She excelled scholastically, and her only school "problem" was that she loved reading so much she would often read during recess rather than play and socialize.

On the flip side, Katie would seemingly push to see just how far she could go before she got into trouble. Yet there was another side to Katie as well. She would seek out those who were disadvantaged or not being treated well by others and befriend them. In short, while Katie could press things to the limit, she also had an incredibly kind heart.

When Katie started to get treated for her mental illness, the medications largely eliminated the stubborn orneriness, leaving a sweet, loving child. At that point, I believe Lauren was left feeling that her role in the family had been usurped by her sister. Let me be clear: neither Anne nor I felt that way, but in retrospect, I'm convinced Lauren did, which was all that mattered. It seemed Lauren felt lost, unsure of how and where she fit into our family.

I gave pet names to each of my kids, and Lauren was "My Sunshine." She brightened my day just by being there. She was always smiling and happy. But around this time, her behavior started to change. Mind you, she still excelled academically and never got into trouble, but her demeanor was less cheerful, and she started to have more problems socially. Some of Lauren's friends no longer wanted to spend time with her, and she had no idea why. She also started to become snippy in the way she communicated at home. Often, her statements were very rude—more from the way she would say things than the words she said.

It's important to point out that before and during this time frame, Anne and I inadvertently did irreparable damage to Lauren. Whenever Katie had a meltdown, Lauren would typically head to her bedroom to escape into her books. At the time, we thought, *Great! Lauren is fine reading on her own.* So, we felt we could focus solely on what was blowing up in our faces with her sister. But many years later, we found out that Lauren had felt abandoned and unloved, as we never bothered to check on her to make sure she was okay.

In truth, we loved Lauren all the more because she could take care of herself that way. We were always grateful for her independent spirit and appreciative of what a blessing she is. But Lauren perceived things very differently and saw this as us neglecting her for her sister.

In hindsight, I should've known better, as my grandfather often said, "To a child, love is spelled T-I-M-E." Unfortunately, there is nothing Anne or I can do to change the mistakes we've made in parenting. All we can do is make sure that we don't repeat them when dealing with our youngest, Sarah. I also hope that by sharing my failures with others, perhaps they will avoid making the same mistakes.

SARAH

Spring 2010

I was squished between Lauren and Katie in the back seat as the SUV glided down the highway. I was the youngest, so I was always stuck in the middle seat. Lauren was her normal moody and quiet self, but Katie was unusually quiet too. I was almost too excited to notice as we approached Westport Plaza to celebrate my ninth birthday at Kobe Steakhouse.

Every year for birthdays, our whole family goes to Kobe, a Japanese restaurant where they cook delicious food on the table in front of you. I always order the meal with shrimp, but you get way more than shrimp. The meals come with everything, from soup and salad to fried rice and noodles. Then, if you pay to get a *bonzai* (which we always do), you get a piece of cheesecake, and the servers sing happy birthday.

We had finally arrived in the parking garage of Westport Plaza, and I couldn't contain my excitement! I skipped all the way to the doors to get inside.

"Calm down!" snapped Lauren. "We're going into a nice place. Stop acting so immature!"

I realized I *should* probably calm down a little bit, but I didn't understand why she had to be so rude. To be honest, Lauren and I never really got along. When I was younger, I would really annoy her, and she would always get mad and cranky. I felt like her "teenage years," as my mom called them, would never end. I was worried she would always be crabby and irritated by me.

Once we entered the building, we got on the elevator and went to the twelfth floor. Once we got to the top, my dad let the hostess know we were there and were waiting for one more person, my Aunt Maggie. She came every time we went to Kobe! Aunt Maggie was amazing, but she wasn't very good at time management—she was always late. Once she arrived, we were seated at a table with a huge stove taking up the center of the long surface.

Katie had been mostly silent the whole ride there and while we were waiting, but I didn't think much of it. I thought she was just tired. Once we sat down, she asked, "Mom, is it all right if I go to the bathroom?"

"Sure, sweetie! Are you doing okay?"

"Yes," replied Katie in a monotone voice.

I began to worry, but I still wanted my birthday dinner to be fun, so I tried not to think about it. Katie came back a few minutes later looking a little flushed and upset. As the night went on, she stepped out a few more times because the hectic and crowded environment at Kobe made her anxious.

Soon after our meal, the servers came to our table with a small drum, candle, and camera. They began to sing happy birthday in Japanese, and I smiled and clapped along happily. Once they finished singing, we all got together for a picture. The servers took the candle away after the picture was taken and replaced it with a chocolate- and raspberry-drizzled slice of cheesecake. We passed the treat around until it was all gone.

Soon after, Katie was wondering when we were going to leave and trying to get my parents to take us home. She didn't like staying at places for very long; she got antsy and anxious.

I often have a hard time not being selfish because on my birthday, I want it to be about me. I don't want Katie to make us leave early or cause anyone to worry; I just want one night for our whole family to go out and celebrate and have fun. Unfortunately, it was always too much for her.

When we finally left, I begged my parents to let us take the scenic outside elevator even though it scared me. Every year, when it wasn't out of order, we would take it down, find our way to our car, and try to leave the parking garage. Half the time, we would get confused and end up going in a circle and laugh at ourselves for never knowing how to get out.

The trip home held less excitement and more worry. Everyone had eaten too much and was starting to feel sick. We all knew Katie was having a hard time, so the whole car ride, we sat in silence as the music played around us, trying to settle our minds and stomachs.

MOM

Summer 2010

During the summer before Katie's first year of high school, her therapist, Brea, informed us that she wouldn't be practicing any longer because she had adopted baby twins. I knew that she had been wanting to adopt for a long time, so I was thrilled for her.

Unfortunately, Katie wasn't so happy. She had become pretty dependent on Brea, and she really struggled to come to terms with the fact that she had to find a new therapist.

At first, Katie tried to remain friends with Brea and would frequently reach out to her. She would even go out and buy outfits for the babies because it's her nature to be so kind and thoughtful. But Brea had to say, "Hey, legally, I'm not allowed to interact with you for a certain period of time. So, this has to stop." That really made it final for Katie, and it was all the more devastating for her.

Frankly, I think this deeply affected Katie and impacted her relationships with psychiatrists and therapists from then on. She tended to have attachment issues, which made it a problem when any of them moved on. Of course, it's not Brea's fault—it's not anyone's fault. This just set the stage for Katie's relationships with future doctors and therapists and taught us how much she needed stability in that regard.

Meanwhile, though Katie hadn't been doing amazing at that point anyway, her mental health started to deteriorate after she found out Brea was leaving, and she became extra sensitive and reactive. Things that would have previously made her angry or sad started to make her *super* angry and sad. This emotional fluctuation gave way to more obsessive thoughts of suicide and pain. It would certainly get worse before it got better.

LAUREN

Summer 2010

Dave & Buster's was as busy and loud as ever. Mom had suggested we go there for lunch as a family. I'd readily agreed,
though I wasn't sure what had prompted her decision. We hardly
ever went to Dave & Buster's—only as a rare treat.

In the car, Mom was particularly quiet. She'd been quiet a lot
lately though. Katie had been struggling most of the summer so
far, crying and self-harming on a regular basis, and it was wearing
on all of us. I gazed curiously at my mom's profile from the back
seat. She'd put makeup on that morning, but it was all gone now.
My stomach twisted with disquiet.

Katie stared out the window, her back hunched and her body
angled away from me and Sarah. It was impossible to see her face.
My disquiet deepened as the pregnant silence in the car stretched
on. I wished Mom would turn the music up a bit louder.

When we got there, we all rushed inside. Mom and Dad picked
out a table right in the thick of the action and sat down holding
hands. Katie remained slightly apart from our family.

"All right, girls. Why don't we eat lunch first, and then we'll give you some money to play games," suggested my mom in a falsely cheery voice.

"Okay!" agreed Sarah eagerly as I looked at my mom in surprise. It was unusual for her to offer up money for something as silly as arcade games. Katie didn't respond at all.

We all ordered burgers, fries, and Cokes. As soon as she finished eating, Katie stalked off. Sarah and I polished our food off soon after and traipsed away more slowly, sticking together as the only ones in the group not looking somber.

"What's going on?" I asked her as soon as we were out of earshot of Mom and Dad. "Is Mom crying?"

"Yeah," said Sarah sadly, looking over at our table where Dad had Mom in his arms. "Something happened last night. Katie and I got into a fight, and she got really mad. I'm not sure what happened after that, exactly, but Katie—"

"She's crying because of me."

Sarah and I both jumped, startled by Katie's sudden appearance.

"What?"

"I tried to kill myself last night."

I stared at her with huge eyes. "What? Why?"

"I was mad," responded Katie in a hollow voice, ignoring Sarah and facing me. "Sarah and I were playing Monopoly, and we got into an argument. Mom came in and saw us fighting and sent us both to our rooms." She paused as tears bulged in her eyes. "I was so mad. I didn't even do anything wrong. She didn't even listen to my side of the story.

"I decided to get back at her. I sat in my room for a long time, thinking about how I would do it. Then . . . I went downstairs and tried to hang myself with my belt. But I couldn't figure out how to make it attach to the ceiling. I tried for over an hour until I got so frustrated that I just hit the punching bag over and over again." Katie gulped, tears streaming down her face thick and fast.

I didn't know what to say. I grabbed her and held her to me, trying and failing to fight back my own tears. She was several inches taller than me by this point and had to bend over pretty far to rest her head against my shoulder, but she didn't let go. "It's okay," I whispered, stroking her hair with trembling fingers. I glanced at Sarah, who looked horrified, her eyes spilling over as well.

"In the end, I went upstairs and told Mom," sobbed Katie against my collarbone. "She was so upset. I hate making Mom cry."

"I know."

"Sometimes I think it would be better for everyone if I would just kill myself so you wouldn't have to keep going through this." Katie shook so hard with grief that my whole body quavered.

"No," I breathed as Sarah stepped forward and wrapped her arms around Katie too. "That would be even worse. I would rather go through this and have you in the end than feel sad every single day of my life knowing that I lost a sister." Sarah nodded in agreement, crying too hard to speak.

In that moment, I was touched by the guilt that my fourteen-year-old sister had to endure. When overcome by the shadows of her mental illness, she did and said things that she didn't mean—things that truly hurt those around her. Once her true self regained control, she had to deal with the repercussions. She couldn't take anything back, but she could never help it either and so was stuck in an impossible position that left everyone feeling miserable.

In the following days, Katie would attend IOP every day instead of school. I would learn that Katie had written a horrifyingly spiteful suicide note that completely went against her true character. I would pull out my kitten and flower puzzle but put it away almost immediately as it provided no emotional relief.

In the middle of Dave & Buster's though, I just held onto my sisters, oblivious to everything else around me.

Everyone's eyes were wet on the car ride home.

LAUREN

Fall 2010

I awoke in the middle of the night, a howling sob caught in my throat. A nightmare had jolted me from my sleep. I was relieved to be awake because my dream, in which Katie had taken herself away from us forever, had felt so unbelievably real.

As I turned the light on in an effort to chase out the remnants of the nightmare, I realized I was crying. It had been so long since I'd actually let myself cry about Katie—about anything. The cloak of darkness outside my window lent me a sense of liberation. Everyone was asleep. I could succumb to my deepest feelings without hurting or alarming anyone. I could wake up in the morning and pretend like it had never happened—like I had never lapsed in my steadfast strength.

With tears still falling, I pulled my dad's old Saint Louis University (SLU) sweatshirt over my head and yanked some jeans on over my pale pink shorts. I was already wearing socks, so I didn't bother with shoes. I just crept out of my room and slunk down to the basement.

Only one of the lights down there turned on. I had to make it all the way down the stairs and across to the other side of the cluttered space to turn on the bare bulb. The darkness pressed on my eyeballs. I was scared, but my fear inspired me. *Katie feels fear constantly. She's scared of the darkness too . . . the darkness inside herself.* Her fear seemed a lot more valid than mine.

As soon as I managed to turn on the light, I allowed myself to truly feel all the pain that I'd been repressing for so long. I choked over broken sobs, holding my stomach as I cried until I felt sick. Finally, after a while, I quieted down, hiccupping as relentless tears continued to broaden the large wet spots on my chest. Rubbing my hands together, I went back upstairs, leaving the light on behind me.

As I crawled back onto my futon, not even bothering to change out of my jeans and soggy sweatshirt, my sadness overwhelmed me again. Allowing myself to lose control one more time, I buried my cheek in my pillow, wondering vaguely just how many tears one body could produce.

Suddenly, the hall light came on, and I immediately tried to stifle my crying, but it was too late. My dad had opened the door, his hair severely tousled from sleep.

"Are you crying? What's wrong?"

"Nothing, Dad. I just needed to have a good cry."

He hesitated, too tired to be sure whether I wanted him to stay or leave me alone. "Okay, then. Good night." He paused, about to turn back to his bedroom. "I love you. I hope you feel better."

"Thanks, Daddy," I sighed, my cheeks still soaking wet, but my tears gradually slowing. "Good night."

MOM

Winter 2011

Although we had loved Dr. Bandi at first, and Katie used her as her psychiatrist for several years, we ended up having problems with her. We would be calling her because we were having a crisis, and she wouldn't answer or call us back. You know, when you're in a crisis mode, you kind of need somebody to respond to you. It was clear she didn't know what else to do for Katie, and we almost felt like she had given up on her. So, we made a decision that it was time to move on to somebody else and get some fresh eyes on her.

It was at this point that Katie started seeing Dr. Barton. He had been recommended by a friend of mine whose daughter was having issues. He had a very dry personality, but he was effective. Dr. Barton encouraged us to begin dialectical behavioral therapy (DBT) with Katie. It seemed like a good idea, and so, my research began!

In the middle of October, we had an appointment with Amina at LifeWork, which specializes in DBT. This program would consist of one hour of individual therapy and two hours of group therapy per week. It sounded ideal. The problem was that it was very expensive, and LifeWork wasn't in our network. The cost was more than we could afford, so my research continued.

Eventually, I ended up discovering Jewish Family Services, which also offered DBT. They had a grant that was provided by the county, so it wouldn't cost us anything, and they had an open spot in the program. Plus, Katie would be able to start seeing a new therapist, Carmen, through this program. All of the stars aligned for us that day.

We began DBT on January 3. Every week, Katie would have an hour-long session with her therapist. Then, on Thursday nights from seven to nine o'clock, she and I would both participate in group therapy. Each group was made up of eight to ten adolescents who were all accompanied by at least one parent or guardian.

For the first fifteen minutes or so, we would do a mindfulness activity, which prompted us to sit and focus on one thing while paying attention to our thoughts and feelings. For instance, my favorite mindfulness activity was coloring. After the activity, we would go around the room and say what we experienced. For example, I may have noticed my breathing or the texture of the crayon.

Next, the parents would all go in one room and talk while the kids chatted in a separate room. Technically, the parents were supposed to discuss the skills they'd used during the week, but none of us really did that! Instead, we talked about the issues of the week and how we'd addressed them as well as what we could have done differently. It was actually very comforting to know that other people were going through similar issues (and in most cases, their issues actually seemed more severe).

At the beginning of the second hour, we would all come back together to learn a new skill that we could practice the next week. I thought most of the skills would be more helpful for Katie; some of them didn't seem like strategies I would necessarily use. But one skill I learned that was very useful was validation. Basically, I learned you can validate feelings without validating the behavior. I also learned that how we communicate is very important.

As an example, "I" statements, such as, "I see that you're very upset right now, and I think we should wait to talk until you have calmed down to talk," are much more effective than "you" statements like, "You need to calm down before we talk about this."

As another example, when Katie was in the third grade, I'd have conversations with her, asking why she would write and say such bad things about herself. I tried to be understanding but also tried to change her mind.

"No!" I'd say. "You're not stupid. You're not fat. Why would you think that?"

But that's not actually validating. Instead, I should have said, "I'm so sorry you feel that way about yourself. I'm sure it's tough to have those kinds of negative thoughts."

I also learned that you should never use the word "but." Instead, you should say "and." For instance, rather than saying, "I know you're upset, BUT you never consider my feelings," you should say, "I know you're upset, AND I hope you can understand that when you yell, it's very upsetting for me." The word "but" invalidates their feelings. "And" is the key to sharing your perspective without canceling out the other person's perspective.

DBT is a yearlong program, but we went through it for two years because Katie still wasn't in a good place by the end of the first year. By the time we finished our second year, we had learned a lot of useful skills. I'm not sure how many Katie was actually using at that point, but she could at least explain the skills to other people. Clearly, she had a basic grasp of each one—she just wasn't necessarily inclined to apply those skills herself. Nonetheless, we both gained important foundational knowledge, and we still try to use those skills to this day.

LAUREN

Spring 2011

It almost seemed like a miracle after how intense everything had been for so many months, but Katie was able to get her medication adjusted, and her mental health improved substantially. In fact, she was almost unrecognizable. We couldn't even remember the last time she had been so happy and healthy. It seemed like she was finally able to lead a fairly normal life.

Of course, she had her moments still. It's not like the mental illness was just *gone*. But overall, she seemed to be thriving more than she ever had before. In fact, she was in an even better place than when she was younger, before she'd been diagnosed. Back then, she'd been so wild, so reckless, so troublesome. Now that she had returned to equilibrium, she was stable and tremendously kind, considerate, and empathetic. It was almost like she didn't have any negative qualities at all. She was just a good kid living a good life.

All was well.

What mental health
needs is more sunlight,
more candor, and more
unashamed conversation.

—Glenn Close

PART 4

LAUREN

Originally Published in Infectus *2016*

NEVER THE SAME

I remember how I felt that day
when you ran out in front of those cars,
your lips tight, face taut, eyes dead,
daring them to crush you.
"That's not my sister," I muttered,
unnerved,
before I yelled at you to come inside.

The babysitter was incensed.
You wouldn't listen.
You were playing with a knife.
"Please stop," I pled,
so unfamiliar with suicide.
You didn't look up.
The sharp blade smirked at me,
smug in triumph.

Why did you have to say that?
Why did you have to get up in front of your third-grade class
and vow that you would slit your throat?
Don't you love me?
Don't you want to play with me anymore?
Don't you like being my sister?

The hospital was a rainbow
with shrieking sobs
and vacant eyes
and groans of delight
souring my stomach.
The air was sweet—suffocating.
These children were raving.
You don't belong here.
Do you?

"Bipolar," they said.
"She's met all the criteria."
I didn't know what that was. I was only eleven.
She would get better.
She wouldn't be the same.

The hiatus was a ruse.
The crazy was still in her,
seizing her body and mind.
It would never leave—
peace, a mirage.

When I was sixteen, she cracked.
She rocked grotesquely on the floor,
sobbing and muttering,
her hands clutching desperately at her ears.
"Get out, get out, get out," she moaned sickeningly,
the image of insanity.

I watched frantically as she surrendered
and disappeared.

I broke myself when I broke her.
Going to college did it.
I thought I was liberated, free to live.
She proved me wrong.
I hated her, and I hated myself.
Maybe I wanted her to kill herself.
Maybe I wanted the rollercoaster pain to sleep.
But that can't be true.
I love her too little and too much.

The guilt and fear burn me up,
slice me apart from inside out.
I cry until I throw up,
tears dripping off my nose, my chin, my clavicle.
How could you do this?
How could you do this?
You are so precious to me.
How can you not see how precious you are?
How can you take yourself away from me?

Twenty-three pills and cuts all up both arms,
but she survived.
I didn't.
I lost my soul to the withering waves of grief
that snap up girls like me
and never let them go.
The fog has frozen my heart
to protect it from her innocent poison.
Love is lost, blinded by anguish.

She will never be the same.
Neither will I.

LAUREN

Fall 2012

My throat was so tight that I could barely rasp out words, but I managed not to cry as I hugged my parents goodbye. They were relatively composed for a couple dropping off their firstborn at college.

The same couldn't be said about Katie and Sarah; they both had tears streaming down their cheeks. Seeing them cry made it even harder for me to maintain control, but I managed to keep it together since there were so many people around. I certainly didn't want to look foolish and weak in front of my new classmates.

Sarah hiccupped when I pulled her into a hug. She usually couldn't stop chattering, but for once, she was quiet. When I put my arms around Katie, she broke down completely, sobbing into my hair.

"I love you so much," she bawled. I took a deep breath to steady myself and rubbed her back a little bit to calm her.

"I love you too, Katie Boo."

Father Curran, the president of Rockhurst University, spoke up from the pulpit of St. Francis-Xavier Catholic Church, breaking us apart. "Again, thank you very much for participating in orientation with us, parents and family. Now that you have said your goodbyes, I ask that you leave us so that the class of 2016 can acclimate to being here and focus on forming friendships. I assure you our new students will be just fine, as they are just about to leave for a service project. Safe travels home, everyone, and God bless."

Family members began filing out of the pews and crowding toward the wide wooden doors in the back of the church. My mom squeezed my hand and gave me a proud smile. "Love you, baby. Call me later."

I nodded, the lump in my throat now making it impossible to speak. Father Curran was talking again, this time just to the new students, but I was still watching my family as they shuffled away from me. Katie's shoulders shook, and Dad pulled her to his side to comfort her. Then, they were swallowed up by the crowd and the closing doors of the church.

As I followed my new friend Ariana out to the buses a little while later, I worried about Katie, the image of her red, tear-streaked face sticking in my head. Almost immediately, I shrugged it off. She was okay; it was just hard to say goodbye. If I was feeling better, she must be feeling better too. After all, *I* was the one who was suddenly thrust into a thrilling but terrifying world of newness, where nothing and no one was familiar.

Katie would surely be just fine. Right?

LAUREN

Fall 2012

When I was younger, I wasn't able to envision Katie's future. After all the times she'd hurt herself—even tried to kill herself—I suppose I just started to feel hopeless. As if this world, including my family and our love for her, would never be enough to keep her here with us. It seemed inevitable that at some point, she would succeed. She would take her own life. No matter how much we tried to keep an eye on her, it was impossible to keep her totally supervised at all times of the day. As sick as it made me, I just couldn't bring myself to imagine Katie's future because I feared she would never get to it.

However, somewhere along the line, I must have started to hope. By the time I got to college, Katie was halfway through high school, and she'd been doing amazing for a couple of years. Katie was smart, talented, kind, and personable. She could do anything—her future was completely open. I truly believed that, and I couldn't wait to see where she would end up.

That burgeoning hope was abruptly doused as I headed off into my future and Katie's future once again became shaky and dark.

I'd had no idea there was anything wrong. I was quite home-sick at the beginning of my college experience. (I'd made some good friends at school, but it's hard to feel totally comfortable with people you've only known for a few weeks.) As a result, I called my mom frequently. Yet I never received any indication that after years of stability, Katie was struggling again.

Before I even went away to college, my mom and I had made a plan for my birthday weekend. I would take the Megabus back home to St. Louis on Friday and spend time with my family that night and all of Saturday. Then, on my birthday, Sunday, September 9, my mom would drive me back to Kansas City. We would spend the rest of the afternoon walking around The Plaza and go out for a birthday dinner that evening.

When that weekend finally came around, I was super excited. I practically skipped out the doors of my residence hall, Chey-enne and Ellie close behind me. Cheyenne—who, incidentally, was the only one of my new group of friends with a car—hopped into the driver's seat of her Jeep, her wild curls bouncing all over her shoulders. I climbed into the front seat, and Ellie climbed into the back. The only one missing from our crew was Rhea, who was still in class.

I used the GPS on my phone to direct Cheyenne to the right place. It seemed like a random intersection with a parking lot on the corner, but minutes later, a blue double-decker bus came into view and settled on the street right across from us. I shouted goodbye to my friends and scrambled out of the car. By the time I joined the queue of waiting passengers and looked back, Ellie had moved to the passenger seat and was waving at me as Cheyenne swung the wheel around to drive away.

Once I got onto the Megabus, I claimed a seat to myself. There were some scary-looking people around me but some nice-look-ing people too. For most of the long ride, I listened to music on my headphones and imagined how happy everyone would be when I came home. Katie and Sarah usually got most of the attention, but I figured one of the perks of going off to college was that I would be the center of everything when I reentered the family dynamic.

It was after 3:00 p.m. when the Megabus arrived in St. Louis outside Union Station. I grabbed my bag and shifted from foot to foot as I waited for the line to move.

My dad was waiting for me beside his car. He didn't say much on the car ride home, but I talked his ear off about school and classes and friends. Though he was practically silent, I could tell he was glad I was having a generally good time.

I quieted down as we turned into our subdivision. I almost felt like crying because I was so happy to be home. I bolted out of the car as soon as my dad hit the brakes and hustled into the kitchen through the door in the garage, my bag thumping against my back.

I don't know what I expected. Perhaps people waiting by the door for me, eager to celebrate my homecoming? Instead, I was met with a heavy silence that stopped me in my tracks. I felt the darkness that blanketed the house and turned to look questioningly at my dad as he came up behind me. In typical dad fashion, he completely missed the look I was giving him. Before I could even say anything, he had brushed around me and stalked off to his bedroom.

Rolling my eyes and scowling at the fact that, apparently, nobody cared I was home, I trudged back to my own room to set my bag down. It wasn't until I'd settled dejectedly onto the uncomfortable futon that served as my bed that I noticed the muted sobbing and soothing responses coming from my sister's room next door.

I sank back onto my pillow and let my mind go completely empty. It had been a long time, but the sound was all too familiar. I guess I should have known there was something wrong when I'd seen my mom's car in the driveway. In my excitement, I'd forgotten that she usually wasn't home from work quite that early.

My meditations were interrupted by the sound of Katie's door swinging open. I jumped to my feet to say hello and see what was going on.

"Get your shoes on, and I'll meet you in the kitchen," my mom was saying in a soft, tired voice. Katie sniffled in response.

I followed my mom to the front of the house. "What's going on?" I asked in a hushed tone. "Katie's not doing well?"

"No," my mom sighed. "She's pretty much been a mess since we dropped you off at school."

I was silent for a moment as my mom hugged me and tried to change the subject. "Why didn't you tell me?" I finally asked quietly.

My mom looked up from tying her shoelaces. "I didn't want to worry you. You're going through an exciting time right now. I want you to focus on your studies and making friends, not this."

This would become a regular argument we had over the rest of my college career. My parents would often act like everything was okay to keep me from worrying, but all that did was make me worry *more*. I ended up not trusting them, so even if they were telling the truth, and Katie actually was doing all right, I just assumed they were trying to shield me from whatever was going on.

In the end, I probably spent a lot more time fretting over it than I would have if my parents had just been upfront with me from the start. I realize they had good intentions, but it definitely strained our relationship and added to my general anxiety and concern. And this was the beginning of that pattern.

"Okay, I get that, but I need to know about this. Katie's my little sister. It's important that you tell me how she's doing, especially now that I don't live here to see for myself."

"Well, you know how it is with her. Every moment is different. I'm sure this will pass soon."

I made a noise in the back of my throat, not quite willing to agree with her.

"Lauren, I'm really sorry, but I'm just not sure that I'll be able to drive you back on Sunday." My mouth fell open. "I know, I'm sorry, but I'm not sure I can risk leaving Katie when she's like this. I already talked to Dad, and he'll be able to take you if I can't."

I dragged in a breath, ready to argue or cry or *something*, but just then, Katie wandered in looking lost and unsure. Mom sent me a surprisingly fierce look for someone so clearly exhausted, and I knew she wanted me to shut up so I wouldn't say anything to upset Katie further. While Mom ushered her out the door, I locked myself in my room and bawled into my pillow.

"Why, why, why?" I whimpered, hands fisted around the corners of the now soggy fabric. "She was okay! How can this be happening again?"

My mom's innocuous words echoed through my brain: *she's pretty much been a mess since we dropped you off at school.*

I buried my face in my pillow again as my eyes burned hotter than ever.

I mostly just stayed out of the way the whole weekend. However, I did connect with Sarah a bit; she was worried about Katie and didn't feel like she had anyone to talk to about it.

"You can talk to me," I told her firmly. "No matter what time of day it is. That's my job as your big sister."

On Sunday morning, the day of my birthday, my mom took me to Bread Co. for breakfast. I told her about school and asked her to tell me everything that had happened with Katie. She didn't say much, just indicated that Katie had been pretty sad, crying and sleeping a lot.

"Please keep me updated," I implored her as we got out of the car, now parked back in the driveway of our house.

"I will. But she's gonna be okay."

"I know." I smiled with a quivering chin.

"All right, are you guys ready to go?" she replied as we closed our respective car doors.

At that moment, my dad popped his head out of the kitchen door to the garage. "You ready?"

"Yes," I muttered. Then, I was in my mom's arms, sobbing into her shoulder. She rubbed my back soothingly, and I wondered if she was crying too. "I'm already so homesick, but this just makes it so much harder to leave."

"I know. But remember, everything's going to be okay. She's really not doing that bad." She squeezed me. "I'm sorry I can't drive you back like we planned."

"It's okay," I mumbled, swiping my fingers under my eyes.

"You'll have fun with Dad though. He has something special planned for you." Her eyes twinkled slightly.

I smiled sadly and got into the passenger side of my dad's car, where I already had my bag waiting for me.

My dad's big surprise was pretty cool. He took me to The Melting Pot on The Plaza once we got to Kansas City. That restaurant was really out of our budget, so we just got the appetizer and dessert courses. It was absolutely incredible, and I had a great time with my dad. Still, I was disappointed. If you have a plan you've been looking forward to for months, it's almost impossible not to be disappointed when it's scrapped, even if the new plan is as good as, or even better than, the original one.

It was almost dark by the time my dad dropped me off at my dorm and made his way back to St. Louis. I must say, my dad really is a wonderful man. He went through a long day of traveling and didn't get home until around midnight, all to make his oldest daughter's birthday special.

When I got to my dorm room, my roommate wasn't there. She was from Liberty, Missouri, so she just stayed with her family most nights of the week. I usually felt lonely and sad when she did that, but this time, I was kind of glad to be alone. I felt more homesick than ever, and now I was worried about my family on top of that.

As soon as I closed my door, I dropped into my desk chair and curled my knees up to my chest. I closed my eyes against the gush of emotions, trying not to let tears leak from under my eyelids. *I have to stay strong, I have to stay strong, I have to stay strong . . .*

Suddenly, there were a few quick raps on my door. Startled, I fell sideways off my chair, somehow landed on my feet, and scrubbed my hands across my face before hurriedly opening the door.

"Happy birthday!" sang Rhea and Ellie, storming into the room with a box of ice cream drumsticks. Before I could contain myself, I dissolved into tears again.

"Whoa, what's wrong?" asked Rhea, standing frozen with the box of ice cream in her hand.

"I'm s-so sorry," I sobbed, mopping at my eyes and trying to regain control. "You guys are just s-so nice to me."

"Well, you don't need to cry about it," laughed Ellie uncertainly, shoving her long, dark waves over her shoulder.

I hesitated for a moment, unsure of what to say. I hadn't wanted to tell anyone at Rockhurst about my sister's mental illness. I just wanted our family to be normal for once. But now my friends would think I was crazy if I didn't give them an explanation.

I sighed. "Look. My sister has a mental illness. She's lived with it since she was eight years old. She's been better for a while, but it looks like she's not doing so well anymore. I didn't know this until I went home this weekend and saw her."

Rhea nodded seriously, listening raptly. "Do you want to tell us about it?"

"It's a pretty long story . . ."

"That doesn't matter," interrupted Ellie in her trademark brusque-but-loving manner. "Here, let's get ice cream."

I spent the next hour telling them about my childhood with Katie and how everything had unfolded. They demonstrated such loyalty and kindness as they listened, the three of us sitting cross-legged on the floor. By the time I finished my story, I wondered why I'd ever considered keeping it from them. I was so grateful for them, in fact, that I decided to tell them what had been burdening my heart since Friday afternoon.

"I just feel like it's my fault," I confessed, getting teary again. "I mean, if Katie can hardly stand a change in the weather, how can she possibly deal with her big sister moving away? She's never *not* lived in the same house as me. Why didn't I even consider that this might be a problem?"

"Lauren," said Rhea, wrapping her small hand around my wrist. "You can't put your life on hold because of Katie. It seems like going to college is an amazing opportunity to get out of that house and be your own person. You can't blame yourself for how your sister reacted. And you can't base your life decisions on her."

Ellie nodded fervently as Rhea spoke.

"I know," I sighed, but I was lying. Many others would try to tell me the same thing over the next few years, and it would be a long time before I'd truly believe it.

MOM

Katie had been struggling for a few months. Ever since Lauren had left to go to school at Rockhurst University in August, Katie had been obsessing on where she would be going to college in a few years. The anxiety continued to creep up, and she was having issues at school. Not issues with getting her schoolwork done—issues with being able to stay in class. Almost every day, she would end up in the nurse's office or counselor's office.

On Monday, we went to see Dr. Barton, the psychiatrist Katie had been seeing for a few years. During this appointment, he informed us that he was moving to Kansas City to be closer to his family. However, he said he would continue to see Katie for another six months and kindly offered to help us transition her to a new provider.

My heart sank, and despair overcame me. I knew that Katie was not going to handle this well. If I knew nothing else, I knew that Katie did not deal well with change—any sort of change. Even changes that were good would negatively affect her.

Recognizing this about Katie, Dr. Barton gave her a prescription for Buspirone that she could take as needed to help with her anxiety. I was hopeful that this would help things improve.

MOM

Fall 2012

That Thursday began like any other day. Katie was feeling very anxious but managed to go to school. I left home early because I had my annual physical scheduled for that afternoon. It was cool and mostly cloudy outside as I headed to work.

Later that day, as I was driving to my appointment, my phone rang. It was Rob.

"Hi there," I answered in a chipper voice. Rob's brief hesitation immediately told me that something was wrong.

"Has school gotten ahold of you?"

"No. What's the matter?"

As he explained to me that the nurse had called to tell him they had just called 911, I began to panic. *Oh no! What did she do!* I had a thousand terrible thoughts running through my head. My face felt numb, and I began sobbing, fear overwhelming me.

"It's gonna be okay, sweetie," said Rob soothingly, trying to keep me from falling apart. "Katie took several pills, but she's alert and doing okay."

Instantly, I felt my panic turn to anger. *How could she do this? Doesn't she know how much we all love her?* I immediately called to cancel my doctor's appointment and raced to Mercy Hospital, the entire time praying to God that she would be okay—asking Him to help us.

Suddenly, I remembered that Sarah would be coming home on the school bus at 2:30 p.m. She was only eleven, and I wanted to shelter her from this for the time being. So, as I raced down Conway Road—and yes, I was totally breaking all the speed limit laws—I called my sister Molly to ask her if she could go to my house to meet Sarah when she got home. As was always the case, Molly was quick to help me and got word out to our family about the situation.

When I arrived at Mercy St. Louis, I could see the ambulance at the door of the hospital. I experienced such a mixture of emotions. I was scared that Katie might not be okay, and at the same time, I was mad that she had taken the pills. I ran into the emergency room and was immediately escorted back to where Katie was. Rob was already there waiting for me. Katie's grade level principal, Mr. Hernandez, and the resource officer were also there. They were very kind and tried to comfort me and Rob.

When I went over to hug Katie, she said she was so sorry and admitted she had taken twenty-three of the Buspirone pills that Dr. Barton had prescribed. I felt so incredibly guilty! I had gotten that prescription filled, given her the bottle, and told her she could take up to three a day. I never imagined that she might try to use those pills to kill herself.

At that point, my anger got the best of me, and I secretly hoped the doctors would pump her stomach so she would think twice about doing that again. But they told us they wouldn't have to do that, though they would need to keep an eye on her for a few hours before sending her over to the behavioral health part of the hospital.

Unfortunately, a little later, we learned that while she would have to be admitted, there were no beds available at Mercy St. Louis.

So, the hospital offered to transfer her to Mercy Jefferson via ambulance.

At this point, we had been at the hospital for hours! It was 5:30 in the morning, and Rob and I had been up for twenty-four hours by then, so we told Katie that we would not be able to meet her in Jefferson County because we needed sleep.

The early morning sun was up as Rob and I walked out of the hospital hand in hand. We were completely exhausted, and we had yet to find out the consequences of Katie's actions from school. It didn't seem like things could get worse, but we were afraid that they would. Only time would tell.

DAD

Fall 2012

I was sitting at my desk, reaching for the phone to call in to an unemployment appeals hearing, when the phone rang. I answered, noting that the call was coming from school.

"This is Rob. Speaking?"

"Hi, this is the nurse up at the high school." She hesitated for half a moment. "Look, Katie is okay, but she just took a handful of pills. The ambulance is here, and they're getting ready to take her to the hospital. I just wanted to let you know what was going on."

"I'll be right there," I replied, a little shocked at what had happened. Before I could rush to my car, I dialed in to the hearing to ask the appeals referee if we could postpone.

"My daughter just attempted to commit suicide and is being rushed to the hospital. I really need the hearing to be postponed so I can go see her, make sure everything's okay," I explained, trying to remain calm.

"How long ago were you informed of this?" the referee asked in response.

"Thirty seconds ago." *Why does that matter?*

"Oh, well, by all means, we'll postpone the hearing. You go take care of your family."

Grateful, I hung up and hopped in the car. While driving, I called Anne, who was on her way to a doctor's appointment herself.

"Did the school contact you yet?" I asked.

"No. What's wrong?" she demanded desperately.

I quickly briefed her on what had happened and explained I was on my way to the school. "There's nothing you can do," I told her, hating how upset she was. "You go on to your doctor's appointment and get that taken care of. I'll deal with everything at school."

By the time I arrived, Katie was in the process of being put into the ambulance. She was crying and apologizing, apparently horrified at what she had done.

Fortunately, the paramedics told me that her vitals were fine, but I wasn't allowed to ride in the ambulance with my daughter.

"Please stay with me," begged Katie, becoming increasingly distressed.

"Don't worry," I soothed. "They won't let me ride in the ambulance with you, but I'll follow and be right behind you the whole way there. I'll see you at the hospital."

Shortly after I got there, Anne arrived. She had decided to cancel her appointment and rush to see Katie as soon as possible. The school resource officer and grade level principal were also present. We were touched that they were so concerned about Katie's well-being.

This wasn't the last time Katie would try to take her life, but it was the first time she overtly carried out a suicide plan. It took Anne and I a while to recover from the shock and fear of the experience, but ultimately, we were just so thankful that we hadn't lost her. We desperately hoped she would get back on track after staying inpatient at Mercy.

LAUREN

Fall 2012

O nce I'd learned that Katie was doing badly again, I started calling my mom even more frequently. She always knew what I was calling for, and she always assured me that Katie was doing okay. Mom didn't give me any details, but since I hadn't seen Katie have a truly hard time for a few years, I assumed my mom's words meant Katie was sad and troubled but generally stable.

Several weeks after my visit home for my birthday, I called my mom. It was a Thursday, and I knew she was at work, but I had some time between classes and a busy night ahead, and I didn't want to forget to check up on Katie. Our conversation went pretty much the same as always. She asked me not to worry, insisting that Katie was fine—maybe even doing better. I hung up the phone feeling reassured.

After that, I had a couple more classes to go to before eating an early dinner with my friends and heading to dance team practice. We had a basketball game that weekend, so I was anticipating an extra-long practice to perfect our halftime routine. Since I figured it might be a late night, I trudged back to my dorm room around 3:15 p.m. after my last class. Grumbling and rolling my eyes, I pulled out the textbook for my music theory class and got to work on reading and taking color-coded notes.

Around four o'clock, my phone rang. I jumped. Then, my stomach filled with dread. Somehow, I just knew something bad had happened. When I turned over my phone and saw my mom's name across the screen, my entire body began to buzz with a panicky feeling. Why would she call me again unless something had occurred? For the first time in a long time, I answered my phone half expecting to hear that my sister was dead.

"Hello?"

"Don't freak out," began my mom in a voice that was intended to sound strong but just came out tired and thready.

Of course, I immediately freaked out. "What happened?" I squeaked, trying to keep my cool.

I heard my mom sigh and knew that she was trying to keep tears at bay so as not to scare me further. I could imagine her face—pale, swollen, makeup almost completely rubbed away due to the constant onslaught of tears.

"Katie took a whole bottle of pills at school today," she finally replied, her voice soft. "They took her to the hospital in an ambulance. It looks like she should be okay, but they're keeping a close watch on her. Once she's cleared as medically safe, they'll move her over to the behavioral health center."

"Okay," I replied robotically, using all my willpower to remain calm for the sake of my mother. "Thank you for telling me. Please keep me updated."

"I will. I love you."

"I love you too."

As though in a trance, I hung up the phone, set it on my desk, and slowly walked into Ellie's room across the hall from mine.

"Hey," she greeted me brightly. "Wait, what's wrong?"

My face had turned red from the pressure of holding it all in, and suddenly, tears were springing from my eyes. "I have to—I have to go home!" I whispered as Ellie stared, her eyes and mouth wide.

"Why?" Her brow furrowed, and she took a step closer, trying to gauge how best to comfort me.

"M-my little sister just swallowed a whole bottle's worth of pills," I sobbed, tears now coming so quickly that I could barely see.

"Oh, honey," said Ellie, taking it in stride. She put her arms around me and let me cry all over the shoulder of her Chiefs T-shirt. "Is she okay?"

"I think so. I don't even know," I hiccupped, drawing away and rubbing my eyes. "I can't be here. I need—I have to go home."

"I know. I would want to go home too. Here, let's look at the train schedule."

"Okay." I darted back into my room and pulled up the schedules for the Megabus and the Amtrak on my laptop. "I already missed all the departures for today," I groaned as Ellie entered my dorm through the open door and came up behind me.

"That's okay. You can go first thing tomorrow. Oh, don't cry," she added as I burst into tears again.

In the end, I purchased the early morning train ticket even though I could have made my only two Friday classes if I had waited for the Megabus. I went to dance team practice despite the fact I was a shaky, red-eyed mess. It was difficult to tell the coach and captain I wouldn't be able to perform at the game and even more difficult to explain why. Luckily, they were very kind and understanding, as were my teachers.

When I called my mom to tell her I was coming home, she tried to encourage me not to. After all, Katie was in the hospital; I was hardly going to see her anyway. Besides, going home wouldn't change anything or help Katie at all.

"But it will help me," I argued tearfully. "I need the support of my family right now."

She was right though. Going home didn't help. Seeing Katie didn't help. To tell you the truth, nothing really helps when your sister is determined to die.

SARAH

Fall 2012

"Katie is in the hospital, Sarah."

Hours before that, I'd been in school with my friends. We'd been chatting about our crushes and the teachers we hated. I never could have imagined that would be the day my sister would attempt suicide.

Katie had been struggling for a little while, but I'd had no idea how serious things had become. As a sixth grader, I didn't always see deeper than the surface. I could recognize something was wrong and that Katie was going through a rough patch, but I thought it would all be over soon, and things would go back to normal.

I was very wrong.

Katie was going through some stuff I would never be able to wrap my head around. My compassionate and loving sister was struggling to understand the worth of her life. Anyone who has met Katie knows that she is a kind soul who always wants to help others. So, honestly, during times when Katie couldn't see how valuable she was to us, it was frustrating. When we looked at her, we saw a smart, caring, and honest individual who had so much to offer to this world. Unfortunately, Katie couldn't always see these amazing parts of herself.

As the bus approached my house after school that day, I saw my Aunt Molly's white car in the driveway. Too excited to worry about *why* my aunt was there, I got off the bus and met her with a grin in front of my house.

"What are you doing here?" I squealed as I got my key out and began to open the door. Our dogs, Sophie and Talley, instantly started whining and barking, crowding around us as we pushed our way into the house.

"We're going to have a girls' night! It's gonna be really fun! We're gonna get our nails done!" I remember the excitement in her voice as she tried to convince me nothing was going on except a fun night out with her and Aunt Maggie.

I have always loved spending time with my aunts, so I didn't give it a second thought. Maybe there was a strange undercurrent to my emotions, as I subconsciously understood that it didn't make sense for my aunts to be there instead of my parents. But I just let myself focus on my happiness at having a surprise girls' night instead.

As Aunt Molly and I entered the nail place across the street from Aunt Maggie's condo, we were welcomed by Ty, one of the owners.

"We're waiting for Maggie, but we're all getting manicures and pedicures," Aunt Molly told him.

I picked out a bright pink color for my nails, while Aunt Molly chose a more subtle pink and Aunt Maggie, who arrived shortly after us, chose a purplish red. As the little polish brushes stroked across my fingernails, I casually asked about where Katie and my parents were. It didn't occur to me that anything too terrible had happened, so Aunt Maggie's response shocked me.

"Katie is in the hospital, Sarah."

I experienced a furious mix of emotions and didn't know which one to focus on. I was angry that no one had told me what was going on until I'd pushed them to. I was worried because I still didn't know what exactly Katie had done or whether she would be okay. And I was upset because I hadn't been able to say "goodbye" or "I love you" to Katie, and I had no idea when she would be back home.

For many years after, when I came home on the bus, I'd look out the window to see if someone's car was there, if I would be coming home to news that something horrible had happened again. Looking out that window every day, I'd feel anxious, wondering whether Katie would be gone again, whether I would get the chance to say "I love you" or "goodbye."

We spent the rest of our "girls' night" in relative silence as I worried over what had happened with Katie. My aunts hadn't told me any details, but my imagination went wild, and I grew steadily sicker at the thought of Katie being hurt.

By the time Aunt Molly took me home, I was so exhausted by my worried thoughts that I just went to bed. I didn't want to spend any more time dwelling on Katie and her problems. It could wait until the morning.

DAD

Fall 2012

Soon after arriving at Mercy Jefferson, Katie ended up fainting and was moved once again to a medical unit. Then, because the medical staff weren't entirely sure what the problem was, she was moved to the cardiac ICU. A neurologist and cardiologist evaluated her and mentioned implanting something under her skin to monitor her heart.

At that point, Anne and I indicated if anything like that was going to happen, Katie would be coming back to St. Louis for it. Shortly thereafter, my brother, Rich, got Katie transferred back to Mercy St. Louis to get another opinion of what was going on.

There was a good reason for this; Rich was a surgeon at that hospital, and he knew the best people to assess Katie. However, she was furious and accused me of being prejudiced against Mercy Jefferson. This would be the start of a long disagreement between me and her regarding that hospital.

Rich was able to get a doctor in to see Katie, and he diagnosed her with postural orthostatic tachycardia syndrome, or POTS. He explained that because of this condition, her heart rate soars extremely high, causing her to faint. We were very lucky that Rich put us into contact with this doctor, as very few were familiar with POTS at that time.

This physical condition, on top of Katie's mental health problems, only served to make things harder for her. She would faint a lot at the behavioral health unit or at school, which created negative attention. This caused her to miss class and increased her stress and anxiety, among other things. Sometimes, she would even bash her head on the ground or table as she fell. It seemed like a curse that someone who already struggled with so much had to deal with this too.

Nonetheless, my daughter is a very strong individual. She learned techniques for keeping her heart rate down and tried her best to be cognizant of the way she was feeling. Of course, over the years, she continued to struggle with her POTS, but she devoted herself to doing what she could to control it as much as possible.

LAUREN

Winter 2013

R hea and I were sitting cross-legged on the floor of her dorm room, munching on some snacks we'd just grabbed from the caf. It was the middle of the afternoon on a Saturday, the perfect time for a heartfelt exchange of thoughts and ideas.

Being as close as we were, we talked about anything and everything that popped into our heads and pushed each other to think about things differently. Though we got along exceptionally well and had similar values, we had very different opinions, so our conversations tended to be spirited and educational. I think we both appreciated this, so we spent a fair amount of our free time engaging in these challenging and thought-provoking debates.

One of my favorite things about Rhea was her strong connection with God. I had long felt distant from my faith as a direct result of Katie's mental health struggles. When I'd been in the sixth grade, I'd thrown myself into my religion, hoping to find solace in God. Unfortunately, the more I learned about Katie's condition and the more I witnessed her fear and anguish, the angrier

I became with Him. Instead of working through this anger, I felt guilty that I would have such negative feelings about God. So, I simply pushed God away, choosing to ignore Him rather than acknowledge my sour feelings.

Despite that, as I grew older, I longed to be close to God and wanted to find a way to work through my disagreements with His "plan." From the start, Rhea helped me with that by bringing God to the forefront and reminding me of His goodness and love. Just talking about Him and sharing her faith and beliefs inspired me and helped me make progress on my own journey.

On this particular afternoon, I finally had the courage to candidly discuss the primary roadblock in my relationship with God. We were deep in a discussion about religion and spirituality, and I felt moved to share the more emotional aspects of my story.

"I don't know, Rhea. I just feel so angry with God for letting Katie have what she has. How could He let her struggle the way she does? I mean, I can understand that terrible things like murder and rape and stuff like that happen because God gave us free will. I can't blame God for that—only the terrible people who commit those terrible acts. But things like mental and physical illnesses or natural disasters or whatever don't have a *reason*. They're pointlessly destructive. Just knowing He would let stuff like that exist makes me doubt Him."

Rhea's response was so simple and so earnest that it almost seemed like it was nothing to her. But it completely transformed the way I perceived seemingly senseless injustices in the world.

"Lauren, you're thinking about it all wrong. It's not that God lets mental illness and all that stuff exist. He would never want there to be bad things like that to hurt his beloved creation. But just like there's good, there's bad. And just like there's God, there's the devil. The devil puts terrible things like that into the world to make people turn away from God—and it worked on you. He got you to turn away from God."

I fell silent, my eyes glazing over as I considered the truth of such a statement. She was *right*. I had fallen for it. The evil of the world had tempted me away from God's light. I felt simultaneously ashamed and relieved. Although I wasn't as zealous in my religion as Rhea, the feeling behind her words resonated deeply with me and kickstarted the relationship that had long been dormant.

This conversation has stuck with me. I still struggle to understand how God could allow Katie to suffer as much as she does, but I always remind myself that God loves me and Katie and all his children. Doubting Him and doubting His love and goodness will only let mental illness and everything it stands for win. Today, I hold strong in my faith, remembering those wise words that fell nonchalantly from the mouth of a wise young girl. Rhea may never know how significant of a difference she has made in my life and my faith, but her influence has helped me more than I can describe.

MOM

Winter 2013

Ever since Katie had been transferred to Mercy Jefferson after taking that bottle of Buspirone, she had insisted that was the only hospital she wanted to go to. And most of the time, she refused to go anywhere else.

There were likely a couple of reasons for that. First of all, Mercy Jefferson definitely had a different feel to it. It just seemed nicer and cleaner to me. So, that probably appealed to Katie. But she also connected with one of the therapists there—Michelle.

Michelle really helped Katie while she was at Mercy Jefferson. There was obviously a strong bond between the two of them, but Katie ended up becoming a little too attached to her. Often, after she was discharged from Mercy Jefferson, Katie would go up and visit her, and they would sit and talk for a while. Ultimately, because of this relationship and her initial experience there, Katie refused to be admitted anywhere but Mercy Jefferson.

Rob and I were very frustrated by this because Mercy St. Louis was fifteen minutes from our house, and the visiting hours were from 6:00 to 7:00 p.m. On the other hand, Mercy Jefferson was fifty minutes away, and the visiting hours were from 4:00 to 5:00 p.m. Rob and I both work, so it was really hard to get there to visit. And, in general, it was just a really long drive to make every day. It got to the point where we ended up saying, "If you want to go to Mercy Jefferson, you need to understand that we will not be able to visit very often. You have to make that choice."

Rob and I actually disagreed a bit on this point. He felt really strongly that Katie should not go to Mercy Jefferson because it was so ridiculous. Mercy St. Louis was obviously so much closer to home and a very good facility. Plus, I think maybe he felt like he had done a disservice to her by not necessarily disciplining her in the years after her diagnosis. So, he wanted to put his foot down and teach her that she didn't get to have everything her way.

On the other hand, my feeling was that Katie was at an age where she could say, "No, I'm not going to go to the hospital." I figured if the only way she'd get the help she needed was by going to Mercy Jefferson, I was fine taking her. So, this was an ongoing discussion among the three of us—one that often created conflict and frustration.

LAUREN

Winter 2013

I was having a blast at college, but things at home were not good. It was distracting to know Katie was struggling so much; I sometimes found it difficult to focus on my classes and extracurricular activities. I did my best to revel in each moment of my college experience because I knew it would fly by quicker than I could imagine, but I was still terribly homesick a lot of the time.

One morning, my mother called me as I was getting ready to go to class. I was busy, so I didn't notice her call coming in, but when I checked my phone a few minutes later, a foreboding feeling stole through me. I called home to check in every day; she only called me when something was wrong.

I bundled up, swung my bag over my shoulder, and began dialing as I swept out of my dorm room.

"Hello?"

"Hi, Mom. Did you call me?" I pushed the door of my residence hall open against the biting wind and shuffled quickly through the cold.

"Yes." She hesitated. *Don't say, "Don't freak out." Don't say, "Don't freak out,"* I thought desperately. "Don't freak out"—I sighed—"but I'm taking Katie to the hospital again."

"What?" I gasped, no longer aware of the icy air. "It seems like she just got out."

"I can't tell you the whole story right now," she said softly, and I realized Katie was in the car with her. "Katie has been self-harming pretty much since she got out of the hospital."

"What? Self-harming? How?" My voice was growing higher pitched as the conversation progressed and my level of alarm peaked.

"She's been cutting herself," Mom responded flatly. Later, I would find out that there was a little bit more to the story than that, but my mom was clearly struggling and probably didn't want to say too much in front of Katie.

I froze halfway up the stairs beside Massman Hall. I was too shocked and angry to find words, but after a while, my mother sighed. "I know it's difficult, but we're working really hard to get her straightened out. I don't want you to worry."

I found my voice, but it was shrill and incensed. "How could she do that?" I turned around and sat down hard on the step above my feet, my left hand covering half of my face.

"Lauren . . ."

"What would make her want to start doing that? Are you kidding me?"

I was interrupted by a bit of rustling coming through the phone. I rolled my eyes, realizing Mom likely wasn't even listening to me. Before I could speak again, she huffed out a breath, clearly gathering her patience. "Katie wants to talk to you."

"What?" I said in a wobbly voice, quite taken aback. "I don't know if I—"

Some more shuffling noises filled my ear. Then, suddenly, Katie was on the other end of the line. I could hear her soft breathing, the irrefutable evidence of her blessed *aliveness*.

"Katie?"

"Hi." Her voice sounded odd. Flat. Empty.

"Why did you want to talk to me?"

"I wanted to say I'm sorry."

"For what?"

"For cutting myself."

Before I knew it, I'd lurched up from the step, leapt back down to the pavement of the parking lot in front of the convocation center, and begun pacing. "I want to say it's okay, but it's not. I can't believe you would do that." I tried to remain calm and keep from sounding too harsh, but I was so angry and emotional that it was difficult. "What would make you decide to start doing that?"

"I just needed to." Her voice was monotone.

"No, you didn't. You did not need to. I bet you got the idea the last time you were at the hospital. I bet a lot of the teenagers in group therapy with you were there because of cutting. Why would you want to imitate them?"

"Because. I was sad, and I wanted to feel pain." Katie's tone had become a bit harder.

Tears slid like frozen dew drops down my face, and I shivered as I continued pacing. "That's stupid," I bit out. "You can barely even feel the pain at the time."

Before I knew it, my mind was flooded with long-suppressed memories of me as a freshman in high school. Bursting with pain but unable to understand it, I had taken up a version of cutting.

Fully aware that I grew faint at the sight of blood, every night, I would take a safety pin and scratch it forcefully across my wrist, gouging a furious line. I remembered tearing at my skin again and again, drawing out the act of cutting, maximizing the pain—but the pain was beyond me. I was aware of it, but it was nothing compared to the pain inside me.

When tiny drops of blood erupted from the wound, I would sigh, trying not to pass out, enjoying the tang of pain. It was a relief to see some physical manifestation of the intangible hurt drowning me internally. The blood made sense; it was a logical result of cutting into my skin. I couldn't make sense of my emotional pain.

After the fact, I always felt guilty and ashamed. I would cover my scratched-up skin with hairbands and carefully hide my safety pins, fearful that someone would find out. Eventually, a couple of my friends noticed, and I was able to gain the strength to stop (partly because my mom forced me to go to therapy after she learned what I was doing).

But still, when I find myself grappling with an emotionally draining situation, I feel the urge to find a safety pin and transform my pain into something palpable. Though I'm glad I never cut more deeply with a blade, it's clear that this was a terrible coping mechanism that only hurt my mental health and sense of security.

"You used to cut, didn't you?" asked Katie without feeling.

"Yes." My voice was tight. "And I know from experience that it didn't really hurt at the time. It only truly hurt after the fact, when I was back in my right frame of mind and I didn't want it to hurt anymore." I stilled and sighed. "Look, I'm angry that you started cutting because I know how hard it is to stop. I only did it for a few months before I stopped cold turkey. But even to this day, I still get the urge sometimes. It just changes you somehow. Not in a good way."

"Well, I went for five days without cutting before today. I wanted to really bad, but I didn't do it until now. I mean, I know it's bad for me to do it."

"Yeah, it's bad," I snapped.

"You can at least be happy that I managed to go so long without cutting. Before this, I cut pretty much every single day."

"I'm not going to be proud of you for not cutting for five days. You went sixteen years without cutting before this."

She hung up on me, and I stifled a sob. What would I do if I'd just upset her enough to make her cut again? Why couldn't I learn to keep from speaking my mind around her, at least when she was stuck in a dark place? My only comfort was that she was going somewhere that would keep her safe from herself.

I walked slowly to my class, hardly noticing or caring that I was fifteen minutes late. All I could think was that I needed to get myself back home as soon as possible.

MOM

Spring 2013

Shortly after Katie began cutting regularly, she was caught at school with a pocketknife, which was what she was using to self-harm at the time. As I later found out, she had cut her leg in the bathroom but accidentally cut too much. Scared of the amount of blood gushing from the wound, Katie went to the nurse's office, claiming to not feel good.

Apparently, the nurse led Katie to a bed behind a little curtain. As soon as the nurse walked away, Katie pulled her sweatpants down to examine her wound, and before she could pull her sweatpants back up over her shorts, the nurse came back over. When she saw the cut, she demanded to know what she had made the slice with. Katie refused to tell her, so the nurse and the school resource officer checked her backpack, where they found the pocketknife.

Keep in mind, school was always a top priority for Katie. So, when she was caught with a weapon, her first concern was that she was going to get in trouble with the school. Katie was worried it would go on her school record and would, in turn, affect whether colleges accepted her.

As you've probably gathered by now, Katie tends to view even small problems as world-ending issues. So, in her mind, this was an utter catastrophe. As a result, she had another huge meltdown, and we decided it was necessary to try inpatient treatment again. But because of her experience at Mercy, we thought we'd try someplace different. We decided to go to CenterPointe instead.

As part of the admission process, they have you sign a form stating that you know the facility is owned by the doctors. Though we had never taken Katie to a privately owned hospital before this point, this wasn't a problem for us at all.

Once Katie was admitted, we returned home, exhausted. I believe it was a Thursday, and the difficult thing is that there's usually not a lot of progress made over the weekend. But, of course, we did go visit Katie on Friday and Saturday.

On Sunday, before we went to visit, Katie called and was very upset. She had been in the shower, and when she got out, the staff was removing a guy from her room. Apparently, this guy had been close to coming into the bathroom where Katie was showering. I don't think this was the first time this had happened, and Katie was scared.

I told Rob that I couldn't do this any longer—I needed to get her out of there. I was heartbroken that she was so terrified! So, we told Katie that we would come and get her.

Katie hung up the phone but called back five minutes later to say she was fine and we didn't need to bring her home yet. It turned out the staff had told her that if we removed her against medical advice, insurance wouldn't pay for any of her stay.

I was furious. *Are you kidding me?! You are going to tell this to a kid who, by the way, is dealing with anxiety and self-harm?!*

Rob called and spoke with the nurse and insisted on talking to the doctor. In the end, the doctor never called us, but the hospital agreed to release her. We decided to NEVER go back to this facility again!

Of course, the fact that Katie had brought a weapon to school couldn't simply be ignored. She ended up being suspended, but it wasn't considered a disciplinary suspension, and it didn't go on Katie's record. Given her extreme concern over how this incident would affect her future, we opted not to tell Katie about this. Fortunately, she didn't even realize she had been suspended because she was in the hospital for a week anyway. So, the repercussions were relatively minimal for Katie, though she certainly wasn't in the clear regarding her mental health.

MOM

Spring 2013

A couple of months after Katie was discharged from the hospital, she went back to IOP so the doctors could continue adjusting her medications and she could receive therapy services daily. In addition, she was being observed to ensure the medications were working.

While Katie was there, her therapist, Carmen, decided to change her career path and go back to school. So, Katie was stuck in IOP until she found a new therapist. This was a difficult situation at first, but it resulted in Katie meeting an adolescent therapist who really changed her life. This therapist's name was Char.

One morning, while anxiously waiting to go into group therapy, Katie noticed a little boy named Paxton playing with some Legos while waiting for his day to start. Since Katie has always loved kids, she started interacting with Paxton, asking him what he was building and getting him excited for the coming day.

After Paxton left to go to his group with the younger kids, Char pulled Katie aside to say that her face had completely lit up when she was playing with Paxton, so she should consider volunteering to work with kids at her church.

It didn't take long for Katie to submit an application at The Crossing. This put her on the path to form lifelong relationships with mentors in the church, to find a meaningful way to work with children, and to accept Jesus into her heart. In many ways, this totally changed her life for the better.

As all this was going on, we knew we had to find a new psychiatrist for Katie since Dr. Barton was leaving. Katie was still attending IOP at this point, so I ended up asking Char who she would recommend. She said if her child had a mental illness, Dr. Bradenton was who she would take her to. Char is absolutely amazing, and I totally respect her opinion, so we made an appointment with Dr. Bradenton.

Of course, we weren't just searching for a new psychiatrist at that time; Katie needed a new therapist too. After almost three months of searching for someone new and receiving counseling services from IOP, Carmen's replacement was hired. Her name was Deanna.

A few days prior to meeting with Deanna for the first time, Katie had psychological testing done at UMSL. It was an all-day process that required Rob and I to fill out paperwork with all sorts of information. Then, we had to complete questionnaires, and Rob and I weren't allowed to talk to each other—or even look at each other—while we wrote down our answers. Meanwhile, the examiners talked to Katie extensively and asked her question after question. Katie even did some testing over the computer.

Four to six weeks later, we received the results. Katie was diagnosed with a mood disorder not otherwise specified, major depression, generalized anxiety, and OCD.

Katie was sixteen when this was done, and like every other teenage girl, she tended to be insecure. That might be why Katie ended up putting too much value in these diagnoses. Basically, she started to let them define her. It was like her diagnoses became her whole identity, and we didn't know how to help Katie recognize who she was apart from her mental illness. This was a challenge we would face for many years—helping Katie see her mental health conditions as a *part* of who she is, not the whole.

DAD

Spring 2013

A s Katie went deeper into her teenage years, she started to define herself based on her mental illness. Everything was about her mental health, and we couldn't have a discussion without talking extensively about it.

As an example, when Katie learned that people with bipolar tend to spend money like crazy, she suddenly started spending money like crazy even though she'd always been extremely frugal. She was just highly suggestible, and she relied on her mental illness to understand who she was as a person.

The way I see it, I have a seizure disorder. I have high cholesterol. And I deal with depression. But if someone were to ask me to talk about myself, I wouldn't bring any of those things up. I would say how old I am, indicate I'm a lawyer, mention I'm married to my high school sweetheart, and highlight some of my personality traits. Yet if someone asked Katie to talk about herself around that time, she would simply say, "I have bipolar, I have depression, and I have OCD." And that would be the end of her self-description. I believe that's defining yourself by your illness, not by who you are. And she allowed herself to do that to such an extent that, in her mind, her mental illness really was all there was to her.

Of course, I never wanted her to feel ashamed of her mental illness. It's a part of who she is, maybe even a big part. But there is so much more to her than that, and I worried she would never discover who she really is if she allowed her mental illness to completely consume her identity.

LAUREN

Spring 2013

I met Jordan at the end of my freshman year of college. We were at a party at White House (an off-campus bungalow so named because it was painted white), and he appeared before me with a beer in his hand and a goofy grin on his face.

"Jordan Green!" squealed Rhea, throwing her arms around his neck.

"Hey. Lauren." I introduced myself in a clipped voice and smiled vaguely at him, not particularly interested in the interaction. Jordan looked like a stereotypical frat boy in his orange shorts, blue polo, and weathered Sperrys. I figured a conversation with him would be about the same as any conversation with a PKA or TKE dude. And I had more pressing matters to consider. Rhea's on-again, off-again boyfriend (who, incidentally, would one day become her husband) was marching through the crowded room toward us, eyes blazing. The drama that ensued swept me away from Jordan, and I didn't see him again until months later.

At the beginning of my sophomore year, Jordan and I became friends of a sort. Basically, he was my drinking buddy. (Now, don't get the wrong idea . . . I hadn't become a wild child by any means, but I did like to have fun on the weekends. It was all part of the college experience, right?) Even though Jordan went to UMKC, he always knew where all the Rockhurst parties were. And whenever he wasn't looking, I was fond of stealing beers out of the case of Natty Lights he lugged to parties.

Over time, our friendship deepened, and we talked every day. I discovered that he knew how to have fun, but there was so much more to his personality and disposition. The more I got to know him, the more I came to realize that he was smart and sweet and enticingly challenging. He wasn't one to say whatever I wanted to hear—he liked to present a conflicting viewpoint and spar back and forth. It was maddening, it was exhilarating, it was exactly what I needed.

We're still not exactly sure when and how we transitioned from being close friends to actually dating, but by the end of my sophomore year, we were pretty exclusive. The luster of fresh romance brightened our eyes and rosied our cheeks, but uncertainty hovered over us. Jordan had just graduated from college and was planning on moving home to St. Louis at the end of the summer. Of course, that was when I would be going back to Kansas City for school—two more years of it.

At the beginning of August, shortly before I was due to return to school, Jordan and I decided to commit to trying long distance. It would be difficult, but it was worth it. And it wasn't like Kansas City and St. Louis were that far apart. We would prioritize spending time together when we could while still leading our separate lives in two different cities.

My parents were thrilled because they'd been so charmed by Jordan's engaging personality when they'd met him. Sarah, who was in middle school, liked him even more than she liked me! The only person who wasn't happy was Katie.

Whenever I came home, I spent most of my time with Jordan. I mean, he was my boyfriend, and I hardly ever got to see him, so of course I wanted to spend every possible moment with him! But Katie grew a little jealous and possessive. Since I didn't have too much of a dating history, she'd never had to share me with anyone before, and she wasn't used to someone else swooping in and stealing my attention. Plus, Katie was still struggling with her mental health at the time, so she would get angry and offended if I missed her hospital visiting hours to be with Jordan.

For a long time, Katie's view of Jordan was tainted by her strange jealousy. She didn't really have anything nice to say about him, and she was pretty rude to him when he came around our house, making Jordan feel like he had done something wrong. I tried to talk to Katie about this, and I believe my mom did as well, but nothing really changed until Jordan and I had been together for over a year and Katie had gotten to really know Jordan as a person.

At that point, Katie began to truly appreciate Jordan. She didn't necessarily know what to say to him, but she'd laugh at his jokes and welcome his presence in our family. In fact, she even expressed to me—on more than one occasion—that she already saw him as a brother-in-law. That was fortunate because Jordan *is* her brother-in-law now!

When Jordan and I began dating, he didn't necessarily know the extent of my family's involvement with mental illness. But he sure found out quickly. Jordan deals with OCD and anxiety himself, so mental illness isn't foreign to him by any means. But he hadn't experienced anything quite as extreme as Katie's difficulties. Even still, he's often startled by the things Katie does and says, but he is trying to understand.

Jordan loves Katie as a sister, which means that he cares for her unconditionally. However, that also means that he gets frustrated with her sometimes, especially when she hurts me. Jordan's top priority is my well-being, and when Katie breaks my carefully constructed sense of okayness, he gets pretty upset. Still, he roots for Katie and is always willing to help her out when she asks.

MOM

Spring 2014

The first half of Katie's senior year went okay, but during the second half, she really struggled—I think because she was so freaked out about almost being done with high school. She went to the hospital several times, meaning she missed school—a significant amount. Then, of course, she would become anxious about all she'd missed, and that anxiety would make it even harder for her to get to school. It was a vicious cycle.

As the end of her senior year approached, it became clear Katie couldn't feasibly finish all her assignments. She was too anxious, and there was just too much to make up. Luckily, the school was very understanding and worked with us to make it more manageable for Katie to get at least some of her work completed. They even ended up letting her skip some assignments provided she could show she understood the concepts. Still, all this impacted her grades, causing her to go from being in the top 10 or 20 percent of her class to below the top third.

Nonetheless, Katie pushed through and graduated with the rest of her class. Rob and I were incredibly proud and, honestly, relieved. She had made it in spite of all she had dealt with.

Throughout this time, Katie had decided she really wanted to go to SLU. Rob and I thought it was a bad idea because it was so expensive, but she worked really hard to get all sorts of grants and scholarships. In fact, she even convinced SLU to give her, as a freshman, a scholarship for social work that isn't normally offered until sophomore year. That made the cost roughly equivalent to Maryville, which is where we wanted her to go because it was less expensive but still near home. So, we felt maybe God was stepping in and we should accept that as divine intervention and let Katie go to SLU. Still, we had serious reservations.

Katie had just purchased a car (against Rob's advice) and had accrued a lot of credit card debt, so even though we would have preferred her to focus entirely on school, she needed to work. To keep up with all her payments, she held three jobs—one as a bagger at Dierbergs, one as a nanny, and one as a caretaker at a daycare center. She tried to juggle everything, but her anxiety prevented her from being able to deal with it all.

Not long into her freshman year, she was cutting, she was fainting, and her anxiety was through the roof. She barely even made it halfway through the first semester before she ended up going to the hospital and had to withdraw. SLU allowed a retroactive withdrawal and refunded all our money, which was very nice of them.

From that point forward, Katie attended St. Louis Community College part time. Half the time, she made it through the semester; half the time, she ended up having to withdraw. Over the course of four years, she accumulated thirty credit hours. Part of those were from Maryville when she was still in high school and received dual credit.

School was difficult for Katie, considering her anxiety and depression, but she never gave up. She always worked hard and started over again. Despite the financial and emotional strain of it all, Rob and I were very proud of Katie for always trying again. She's a strong girl, and she never stopped proving that, even in the midst of her mental health challenges.

LAUREN

Fall 2014

Katie was in and out of the hospital an alarming number of times during my four years of college. She was once in the hospital as many as four times in eight months.

I was a dedicated student who earned high grades, participated in many volunteer opportunities, and was involved in countless extracurriculars and honor societies. I was determined to graduate with a 4.0 grade point average and a rainbow of cords around my neck. But as far as I was from the tumult at home, I was still smothered by it—and it showed.

Each time Katie tipped over the precipice, I rushed home, desperate to be there even if there was nothing I could do. I left the dance team in the lurch for basketball games, missed meetings, work, class. I put my goals on the line to be there for my family (in spite of their insistence that I stay in Kansas City).

I didn't realize how much it was all wearing me down until my junior year, when I informed my social mentor facilitator, who also happened to be one of the university counselors, that I had to miss a steering committee meeting because my sister was in the hospital again. In his cool, calm voice, he let me off the hook for the meeting but asked me some questions I couldn't answer at the time:

"What are you gaining by going home? What difference does it make? It won't change what's happening. I know you want to be there for your sister and for your family, but I've watched you struggle to keep from unraveling, constantly going back and forth. I think you need to challenge yourself to *not* go home and see how that feels. Your life and your needs—outside of your sister's—are important too."

Though I knew he had a point, I resisted. "I understand that, but I don't just go home for them. I go home because I need to be with people who love me and understand and can make me feel better." I paused, thoughtful, slightly defiant. "I mean, if my grandpa had a heart attack, I would go home to see him even if I knew I couldn't do anything to help. I would want to be there with him, see with my own eyes that he's okay."

I stubbornly went home on that occasion, but after that conversation, I finally let myself focus on my own needs a little more. And though I did go home to visit Katie in the hospital whenever my schedule allowed it, I stopped sacrificing my own commitments every time she had to go to the emergency room.

Because my social mentor facilitator had helped me get my mind in the right place, I decided to continue confiding in him. He wasn't allowed to actually be my counselor because that would have somehow been a conflict of interest. But he did do what he could for me, which was extremely kind of him considering I didn't have a lot of patience for therapy and counseling, believing that talking about my feelings didn't really help anything.

To be clear, I think that therapists and counselors are super helpful. Katie could never have gotten as far as she has without them, and I have a deep appreciation for their skills in general. But because my meager experiences with therapy and counseling hadn't made a meaningful difference for me at the time—possibly because I hadn't put my full effort in—I was skeptical.

That's why it was such a big deal when my social mentor facilitator showed me that therapy and counseling have the potential to be effective. This was my first step in the right direction regarding coping skills, and I'd like to think I have only improved since then.

SARAH

Throughout my middle school years, there was so much going on with Katie all the time—it was constant. When she ended up in the hospital, I'd be overwhelmingly scared and upset. Day to day, when I was coming home from school, I'd feel anxiety form in the pit of my stomach.

Is she gonna be home? I'd worry to myself. *Did she do something? How's tonight gonna go?*

This happened every single day. And I would be distracted during school 'cause I'd be worried about what was going on at home—what was going on with Katie.

Katie and I have always been pretty close. Growing up, she was one of my friends, kind of like a second mom. When I was little, we'd play house and other games together, and she was always there for me. One reason why we were so close could be because I've always put me and Katie's relationship first. I felt a responsibility to ensure she was okay.

Back then, the three of us sisters didn't get along very well, so we would get into arguments. Whenever that happened, I would get really worried about Katie's mental state and usually take her side. Otherwise, I'd immediately go to Katie to check on her because I was concerned that any little thing would trigger her to self-harm.

Honestly, as a little girl, I didn't really understand what was going on, so I didn't have as much of an emotional reaction to Katie's mental illness. Typically, my response would be confusion. I recognized something was wrong, but I didn't know exactly what it was because Mom and Dad wouldn't talk about it very much . . . at least not to me. So, I'd always just try to keep things on an even keel. Whenever I *did* cause issues, I would apologize, even if I didn't really do anything wrong. I always wanted to sacrifice things for Katie's sake, so the two of us tended to be closer compared to me and Lauren.

However, as I got older, I realized that even though Katie has a mental illness, she needs to learn that she doesn't always get her way. So, I began to go to Lauren and make sure she was okay first—or at least make it more even. I still felt scared Katie would do something, but I realized that she can't use that as an excuse or a means of manipulating people.

When I was in the third grade and Katie started having more serious problems, I had to deal with some adjustments. I remember thinking it was going to go right back to normal once she got better. I figured we'd be playing house and hanging out like always. But that's definitely not how it went. Katie was a different person, and it was difficult for me to understand that.

Unfortunately, these changes put a strain on our relationship, and the distance grew between us. Suddenly, Katie didn't want to do things with me anymore because she wanted to be more independent. I'd become her annoying little sister, and she decided she didn't want to spend as much time with me. At that point, I was on the back burner for Katie, and since I felt like I wasn't really close to Lauren either, I was pretty upset—and pretty lonely.

Luckily, once I approached adolescence, Katie and I became close again. I would hang out with her all the time, and we would joke around a bunch. When she was having hard times, I could usually get a smile on her face by goofing around with her. I think we found a way to connect through our humor, and we used that as a healthy coping mechanism. So, when Katie was struggling, we would just drive around and scream the lyrics to songs and things like that. I'd be silly with her just to cheer her up. I cherished this relationship.

A couple of years later, once I took on the teenage angst Lauren had left behind, I would become tired of the constant struggle and how it was never better. So, I'd start to draw away from Katie because I felt more mature and got frustrated by the things she found funny. Basically, I would decide I was too cool for everyone. At that point, that joking type of relationship we had would largely fade away, making Katie feel like she had done something wrong.

But as a young high school freshman, I simply enjoyed joking around with my big sister. Although she was in and out of the hospital almost constantly, I still had hope that she would get better.

MOM

When Katie hurt herself or tried to take her life, I would often get mad.

When she'd been younger, it had been easier for me to be more sympathetic and loving. After all, as a parent of a young child, it's natural to be caring and nurturing because they're relying on you, and you want to help them.

But at this point, when Katie was an adult and was still constantly cutting and attempting to kill herself, it was hard not to give in to the anger. And Rob was struggling with it too. It was just hard *not* to be furious at the thought of Katie trying to take herself away from us.

In order to deal with this, we ended up taking some family therapy, and through this, we discovered that this anger is actually a secondary emotion stemming from fear. When I learned that, it made total sense. Every time Katie punched the wall, cut herself, or took a bottle of pills, my thoughts would alternate between the two emotions. I would think things like: *What if, God forbid, she hadn't gone in and gotten help after she took those pills? She'd be dead.* That's what scared the hell out of me (emotion number one) and made me mad (emotion number two). *Like, why are you doing this? Stop it.*

I felt so guilty for feeling that way because it seemed so wrong, but now, looking back, I think that's a normal reaction. You want to tell somebody who's doing these things, "*Just stop it!*" But that doesn't help, obviously. It's a mental illness. That's not how it works.

That's the difference between raising a child and raising a child with a mental illness. Once your kid's an adult, the normal course of things is for them to grow independent and grow away from you. That all still happens with someone living with mental illness, but there's plenty of dependency remaining.

Katie tries to break away, but she still needs me. It's very frustrating sometimes—for both of us. Even still, I wonder, *What's she going to do when I'm not here?* She has to figure these things out on her own. This is an ongoing process—even to this day.

SARAH

Summer 2015

During the summer between eighth and ninth grade, I went to lunch with my elementary school counselor, Mrs. Singer, and her infant son at the Pasta House right up the street from our house. She asked how I was doing and how things were going with my family. I told her that things were going well in my world and that Katie was doing so much better. I felt relieved that I didn't need to constantly worry about Katie because she was doing so well. After we finished eating, she drove me home. I intended to have a nice, relaxing afternoon; however, that didn't go as planned.

A few hours after I got home, Katie got into a heated argument with my parents. Apparently, Katie had been doing much worse than I'd thought. Her therapist, Deanna, had just left, and she had gone downhill very quickly, even though she had started seeing a new therapist, Kelli. Katie felt that she needed to be placed in the hospital and wanted to go to Mercy Jefferson instead of Mercy St. Louis. My parents, on the other hand, felt that they could keep

Katie safe at home and thought she didn't need to be put into the hospital at all.

While they were arguing about where she should be during this time, home with her family or at the hospital, I was in my parents' room. I sat on the floor next to my mom's side of the king-sized bed, looking out the window and listening to them fight. I was crying and just wanted everything to be okay again.

After a while, I called Lauren. My parents never wanted me to call her because they thought it would make her too stressed out when she needed to be focused on her schoolwork. In fact, one time, I'd called Lauren after Katie had had another breakdown, and in the middle of my call with her, my dad had yanked the phone out of my hands and yelled at me for distracting her when she was supposed to be studying for her finals.

Back in this moment, Lauren tried to calm me down and find out what was going on. Although I was scared and upset, I made an effort to explain everything that was going on as voices continued to rise in the other room.

"You need to do something to distract yourself from what's going on. Listen to music or something," she suggested.

"They're yelling at each other. I would hear them over any music."

"Then, get out of the house and go on a walk."

I considered it but was too scared to go into the family room, where they were, to leave. Plus, I felt like I couldn't leave without telling Mom and Dad where I was going.

"Oh, don't worry about that. Mom and Dad will be understanding given the circumstances. You clearly need to get away from all of the fighting."

"You know what? You're right." I hung up and ran into my room to grab some socks and tennis shoes. As I was putting them on, I heard feet coming closer to my room, more shouting, and then something shattering. I rushed to put my other shoe on and hurried out into the hallway, hesitating when I saw a picture frame smashed into a million pieces on the floor. I ran down the hallway and started toward the front door.

"Are you okay?" asked my mom distractedly, her voice startling me.

"I'm fine. I'm going on a walk."

I finally got outside and took a deep breath. When I called Lauren back, I told her what had just happened as tears poured down my face. I was so scared. Katie had gotten upset before, but she rarely became hostile. Lauren got me to calm down, and I started to walk home after I'd stopped crying and finally felt a little better.

I was almost back home when I saw my dad outside looking for me. My parents always had to be with Katie during a crisis. I was okay with that because I knew she needed them more than I did, but it meant a lot to me that my dad had left her with my mom and gone to come find me to make sure I was okay.

Together, we walked inside, lost in our own thoughts, united in our concern for what was to come.

MOM

Spring 2016

T he week before Lauren's college graduation, Katie was having issues, so I spoke with Michelle, the therapist from Mercy
Jefferson who Katie was so attached to. While Katie did need to
be admitted to a hospital, Michelle and I both agreed that it was
not a good idea for Katie to come back to Mercy Jefferson because
of the relationship that had formed. It had ended up crossing the
boundaries of what would be acceptable between a therapist and
patient.

Nevertheless, Katie insisted on going there. She was assessed
in the ER and told that there were no beds available.

"Are there really no beds? Or are we just being told that
because of the situation with Michelle?" I asked the social worker
outside Katie's room.

"Michelle told us to tell Katie there were no beds, so that's
what we told her."

While I understood the sensitivity of the situation, I was also frustrated because my daughter seriously needed some help! So, since I was concerned about Katie's mental state and worried she might hurt herself, I spoke with Dr. Bradenton. I needed to get her admitted somewhere.

We ended up getting her admitted to Mercy Jefferson. Michelle was not very happy about that, and Katie knew she had been lied to because there were plenty of beds when she got up there. That was the last time Katie insisted on going to Mercy Jefferson.

Katie stayed inpatient there for several days. Rob and I were actually hoping that she would be kept over the weekend so we could be sure of her safety while we were in Kansas City for Lauren's graduation. But we weren't certain that would be the case, so we drove her car up and left it in the parking lot so she would have a way to get home if she was discharged. (Everyone in the family except for my mom, who was too old to travel, was going to be at the graduation also.)

Shortly after we left for Kansas City, Katie called. She had been released, much to our chagrin. We just told her to call Grandma and stay with her while we were gone for the weekend.

Rob and I had decided that we were going to Lauren's graduation no matter what. We had come to the conclusion that if Katie was discharged while we were gone, there was nothing we could do, and hopefully, Katie wouldn't make the poor choice to hurt or kill herself. But we had agreed that if she did, we couldn't feel responsible for it.

Of course, if she had ended up killing herself, we would have been torn apart over it. But we felt that we hadn't been there for Lauren before, and graduation was a big deal that Lauren had worked really hard for. There was no way we were going to miss it.

LAUREN

Spring 2016

The week of my college graduation was one of the best weeks of my life. I had worked so hard throughout my academic career to prove myself as a student and professional. While working two part-time jobs and participating in close to a dozen school organizations, I had fought to maintain a perfect 4.0 GPA over four straight years.

Now that school was over, the sense of freedom and anticipation was dizzying. I was slightly worried that I had gotten less than an A on my senior capstone or my senior thesis (I had double majored), which would have been frankly tragic for a perfectionist like me. But I had a few days to revel in my adultness before I had to worry about that.

During that glorious week, I attended Rockhurst's first senior retreat. It was such a reflective time for me, and I felt, more than ever, that I had gained everything I had wanted—and more—from my Jesuit university experience. Then, the next day, Rockhurst took the seniors to Worlds of Fun on a party bus. We all felt so giddy and close after all we had achieved as a class. We skipped from roller coaster to roller coaster, laughing easily and throwing our arms around each other in affection.

Our special senior activities were amazing, but I knew the best was still to come. While waiting for my parents to arrive, I decorated my graduation cap with "Words are our most inexhaustible source of magic," uniting my love of *Harry Potter* and future career plans in one sparkly sentence. Then, antsy with excitement, I wandered outside my on-campus house and planted myself on the stone wall separating the front walk from the lawn.

Dozens of cars came by, and I cricked my head around every time I heard them approaching until, finally, it was my mom, Dad, and Sarah parking out front.

My heart leapt with joy, and I flew down the front steps, beaming at them.

"You're here!" I squealed, giving my mom a hug. "I'm so happy!"

"Hello!" she laughed, a little surprised by my fervor.

The truth is I was a little relieved they had actually shown up. Leading up to my graduation week, my mom had called to tell me that Katie was doing poorly. Then, just a few days prior, she had been admitted to inpatient again. Accustomed to being pushed to the side for the sake of Katie and her mental illness, I'd felt my throat clog up and forced myself to be quiet and calm.

"Are you still going to be able to come?" I'd asked as nonchalantly as I could manage.

"Yes, of course!"

That response had given me pause. I was overcome with relief, but I still doubted it somehow. And I was shocked that my mom was so firm in her resolve. I had never really experienced my family choosing me over Katie before. It had always been Katie first, everything else second.

Seeing my family crowded around me on the sidewalk in front of my house in Kansas City made me almost drunk with happiness. I ran around like a wild woman, full of energy and life. I was probably pretty annoying, being everywhere at once, but I just couldn't contain my high spirits. Everything was working out!

The next morning, I filed down the aisle with the rest of my class, kind of in denial about the fact that college was over. As I settled into my metal folding chair somewhere in the middle of the sea of students, I turned my head this way and that, trying to find my family and Jordan, but the arena was far too big, and I couldn't recognize anyone.

After the national anthem and some inspiring speeches, it was time for the president's honor award to be announced. I waited with bated breath, crossing my fingers . . .

". . . and Lauren Green are receiving this award for graduating with the highest grade point averages of the 2016 class. Congratulations!"

I stumbled to my feet and briskly walked up to the stage to join the other classmates who had won the award with me. It was so unreal that after all that time and effort, my objective had been realized. My heart felt so full and warm as I waltzed back to my seat. I had really done it!

As the announcer started calling the names of my classmates in alphabetical order, I glanced around, searching fruitlessly for my family again. I could feel their pride from where I was sitting, and I wanted to see it on their faces.

After what felt like forever, it was my turn. My row stood and walked in a line to the base of the fold-down steps. Then, one by one, we crossed the stage to receive our "diploma" (the real one would be mailed to us) and pose for a photo with Fr. Curran. I had graduated summa cum laude. My academic career had officially come to a close.

Once the graduation ceremony was over, I loitered at the edge of the lobby for a few minutes, waiting anxiously for my family to exit the gymnasium . . .

"Lauren, you did it!" My mom grabbed me and hugged me so hard I thought I was going to choke.

"We are so proud of you, Sunshine," my dad said gruffly. I knew it was because he was about to cry. (He had bawled like a baby throughout the ceremony.)

"Good job," laughed Sarah, giving me a high five.

"Thanks, guys!" I beamed as Jordan put his arm around my waist, silently conveying his pride and support. "Are you ready to walk?"

We all filed outside to join the "Hawk Walk," a procession of graduates from the convention center to the Power and Light district a few blocks away. I found some of my friends and walked with them, my family lagging slightly behind. As a group, we were in a great mood, hugging and taking pictures and throwing our caps high into the air.

After carousing for the rest of the afternoon, we headed over to a nice restaurant located in the heart of Power and Light. I sipped wine and opened graduation gifts while chatting happily with everyone. For what felt like the first time, it was really all about me. It was the most amazing feeling to be surrounded by people who were there in celebration of me and my accomplishments.

When I was halfway through my grilled salmon, my mom's phone rang. I saw a troubled look flash across her face before she stood and walked a few feet away, her phone to her ear. I felt my heart clench, thinking sadly of Katie. She had just gone home from the hospital and was probably not sure what to do with herself without my parents around.

"Sorry," said my mom as she returned to the table, clearly wearing a brave face.

"Was that Katie?"

"Yes."

"Well? What's wrong?"

My mom sighed. "She's having a really hard time right now. I told her she really needs to go to Grandma's like we had agreed. I'm not sure she should have been released from the hospital."

My head drooped and my gaze cast downward. "Do you need to go home? It's okay if you do. I understand."

"No," my mom said so resolutely that I looked up. "You have worked your entire life to get to this moment, and I am not going to let anything stop me from celebrating that with you. Your father and I have chosen to go help Katie instead of being there for you enough times. This time, we're here for you. We'll see Katie tomorrow when we get home. Grandma can look out for her for now."

"Okay," I replied softly, torn about how I felt. Of course, I was thrilled that my parents were putting me first for once, but at what price? We would soon find out.

MOM

Spring 2016

Upon returning from Lauren's graduation, I learned the ugly truth of what Katie had planned to do.

Before she drove to my mom's after being discharged from the hospital, she had taken a shower and gotten lost in her thoughts—dark thoughts. She couldn't stop obsessing over what had happened in the hospital, where her life was headed, and how she was going to make it through the rest of the day. Of course, she was alone at home with no one to hold her accountable to go to my mom's, so she had ample opportunity to come up with the final details of a suicide plan.

As I discovered after talking to a tearful Katie, she had known she would overdose on Wellbutrin since reading how many she would need to take for the plan to be successful. She'd been holding on to this information for a while. However, she didn't have all the pieces of her plan defined. She knew where she wanted to do it, but she didn't have a when. But that day, as she stood in the shower, she made a decision.

May 18. Her birthday.

Apparently, Katie had thought about how people tend to mourn more on birth dates and death dates. She figured if it all happened on the same date, there would be less remembering and less grief for her family.

The next day, May 17, around three o'clock in the afternoon, Katie was at church when Charisse, a pastor at The Crossing, showed up and saved Katie's life. She started talking to Katie and eventually came right out and asked: "I've never seen you like this, and I'm worried about you. I need to know . . . Can you keep yourself safe?"

Unable to lie to someone she looked up to, Katie broke down and confessed what she planned to do. After offering Katie the comfort and support she needed to make it through that moment, Charisse called Rob to let him know what was going on.

We had just arrived back home from Kansas City, so we met Katie back at the house and drove her straight to the hospital. We still had hope for her future, but Katie seemed to have none left. She didn't care which hospital she went to because she believed everything was so hopeless that it didn't matter.

It broke my heart to see my girl like that! What could we do to convince Katie that her life was worth living? How could we get through this as a family when it seemed like Katie's mental illness just wouldn't let her go?

You don't have to control your thoughts; you just have to stop letting them control you.

—*Dan Millman*

PART 5

SARAH

Summer 2016

Dear Katie,

You are constantly telling me how much you love me and how cool you think I am, yet you don't believe me when I tell you those things. I love you more than you could ever imagine! Sometimes I get mad at you, but we are sisters, and that is inevitable. Nothing you could ever do will make me stop loving you and fighting for you. I need you in my life, so you can't give up. Whenever you even think about giving up, look at this letter and convince yourself to keep fighting, even if you don't want to. In this letter, I am going to tell you why I need you, but don't forget that there are many others who need you in their lives too. You may not see how many people you affect, but I do. You are loved and cared about by more people than you even know.

I need you because I need my best friend to be there for me for the rest of my life. I have friends at school, but they won't be there forever. You'll be there for me though. You know what's great about having your sister as your best friend? Well, there are actually a lot of reasons, but to start off, no matter how much we fight, we always make up. Also, you don't judge me, so I can tell you anything. With you, Katie, I know I can say anything because you will still support me, no matter what. I am so lucky to have a sister who is unconditionally loyal, loving, and kind-hearted. Often, you try to express how much you love me, and I just wish you could understand that—and more—is how much I love you.

My absolute favorite thing about you is your humor. Sometimes I'm not in the mood for it, or I feel it's the wrong time for it, but I always appreciate it. I remember one day when I was in my room doing something and you were going through a rough spot. I heard you in the other room playing with the dogs, just laughing your heart out. I could feel the smile on your face, and I just sat down on my bed and listened to you laugh for a little bit. I hadn't heard you laugh like that in so long, and it brought me an enormous amount of happiness. Sometimes, it's just the little things you do that make my day, even if you don't realize it.

I know I've been changing a lot this year and have grown apart from you in a lot of ways, and I'm really sorry. I've been overly stressed by school and other things, and I've started to do things on my own more. But I am quickly learning that I've been naïve, and I truly need you.

When you're struggling, it's hard for all of us, which I know you've heard many times. However, have you heard that when you're doing well, it impacts all of us positively as well? You have impacted my life—all our lives—in such an amazing way that you cannot possibly understand. I never want you to forget your worth, Katie, because to me, you are priceless.

I love you more than you will ever know.

Sincerely,
Sarah

LAUREN

Fall 2016

A faint vibrating broke through the thick fog. I fumbled around in the darkness, my eyes drooping, my ponytail lopsided.

All I heard when I pressed the phone to my ear was loud wailing. "Sarah?"

"Lauren!" She was so hysterical that that's the only word I could distinguish with any certainty.

I was abruptly wide awake. "Sarah! Calm down, okay? I can't understand you. You have to calm down so you can tell me what's going on."

Sarah took several deep breaths, still sputtering loudly. Finally, she was able to speak, though her voice was much higher and thicker than usual. "Lauren, I'm scared."

"Why? Tell me what's happening," I demanded urgently.

"I think Katie hurt herself." Her voice juttered and jumped, and I figured it was just a matter of time before she succumbed to tears again.

"Hurt herself how?"

She hesitated, collecting herself. "Well, when Katie was in the hospital, Mom said that she would take her to The Melting Pot when she came home. So, we went there for dinner tonight. And . . . I don't know. Mom started talking about some stuff, and Katie got really upset. Then, when we got home, I was gonna go to the bathroom, but she was in there, so I just waited. But . . . She was in there for a super long time, and when she finally came out, she just ran real quickly to her room." She suppressed a frightened sob. "I heard her saying 'Oh no. Oh, God.' I think—I think she might have cut herself really bad."

"It's okay, Sarah. It's okay," I said comfortingly, though my stomach twisted unpleasantly. "Did you tell Mom and Dad?"

"Y-yeah. Dad's in there talking to her now. And Mom's—"

Suddenly, I heard shouting in the background, and Sarah's renewed sobs whisked away her words.

"What's going on? What's happening?"

Sarah blubbered incomprehensibly for a few seconds, but finally, she was able to form meaningful words. "She's yelling at Mom that it's all her fault. She's blaming *Mom* . . ." Her tears rendered her speechless again.

There was a confused shuffling sound, and I heard muffled voices speaking back and forth. Then, quite abruptly, it was my mom on the other end of the line.

"Hi. It's Mom." Her voice wavered, and tears immediately sprung to my eyes. It's never easy to hear your mom cry. "I'm sorry you're having to deal with this. Katie just cut herself a lot deeper than she meant to, so Dad's taking her to the hospital to get stitches." She paused. "It's all my fault. Please try not to worry too much about it."

"It's not your fault, Mom," I said fiercely, rubbing my eyes dry.

"It . . . it is my fault. I was drinking wine at dinner, and I started talking about things I shouldn't have ever brought up." She sounded so exhausted. So defeated. "You should go back to bed, okay?"

"Are you sure? Do you need me to come help with any-thing . . . ?"

"No, no. Dad's taking Katie, and the rest of us are going to sleep." Her voice was colorless, and I knew she wanted some time to herself so she could cry in peace.

"Okay," I responded softly. "Is Sarah okay? Can I talk to her?"

"Yeah. Here she is."

"L-Lauren?" Sarah's voice wobbled dangerously.

"Hey, it's all right. Katie's gonna be fine."

"I know, but . . . It was just really scary. And I just can't believe she was so mean to Mom."

"I know. Me neither," I agreed, my voice hardening in anger. "After everything Mom has done for her. I can't believe that she would do something like that and then try to make Mom feel guilty about it. I don't think she's ever been so hateful before."

The truth is Katie has always been such a caring and compassionate individual, but when in the grip of her mental illness, she turns into a completely different person. She becomes snappy and irritable for no reason. While she's always pretty sensitive, she becomes extra touchy—to the point that we all walk on eggshells, afraid to say the wrong thing the wrong way. And though she's very other-oriented when she's herself, if she's having trouble with her mental health, she becomes, frankly, selfish. She expects everything to revolve around her, and if we don't fulfill those expectations, we clearly "don't love her enough."

That personality shift is alarming, of course, and it was in full effect that night. Yet it's even worse when she's admitted to inpatient at the hospital. Katie is a very mild and agreeable girl who generally avoids conflict and shies away from violence of any kind. But at the hospital, she's been known to act very aggressively toward the other patients. Not only that, but she'll challenge the authority of the nurses and techs, sometimes becoming so angry she punches a hole in the wall or makes nasty threats. One time, she ran to her room, barricaded the door shut with her mattress, and scratched at her arms, desperately trying to draw blood.

Katie would *never* have done anything like that at home. It's almost like she lets the illness inside of her take over when she's in that environment. Maybe it's because she knows she's safe there. Maybe it's because she feels *unsafe* there. Maybe it's because she's away from her loved ones. Or maybe it's because that strange, sterile environment yanks her mental illness out into the open. If that's the case, perhaps it's really a blessing. We can't fix what we don't understand, right?

Anyway, even though Katie becomes ugly like that because of her mental illness, and we can't exactly blame her for her words and actions, we still have an emotional reaction. We're human, and we can't help but feel hurt, upset, and even angry. And that's what Sarah and I were struggling with at that moment.

"Yeah," hiccupped Sarah. "I just can't help feeling mad at her. I don't know why she did that."

"I know, kiddo. Look, why don't you get ready for bed and lie down, okay? You'll feel a little bit better in the morning. Everything will be all right."

"Yeah, okay."

"Love you, kid."

"Love you too. Bye."

I stayed awake for a long time after that phone call, flipping this way and that under my covers. Unwelcome visions of Katie's mutilated arm kept burning the backs of my eyelids, and when I finally did fall asleep, my dreams were filled with blank blue eyes and pools of blood.

MOM

Fall 2016

I had a coupon for The Melting Pot and thought it would be a fun last-minute thing to do with Katie and Sarah. Everyone was in a great mood, and we had a really nice dinner. And then . . . I said something I probably shouldn't have.

Rob got up to use the restroom before we left, and I mentioned I was concerned about whether all Katie's providers were treating her for the same issue. I figured that if they each thought she had a different diagnosis, her overall treatment probably wouldn't be very effective.

When Katie wondered what I was talking about, I mentioned that the doctor from the hospital and her therapist thought it was possible she had borderline personality disorder. This completely set Katie off, and she became extremely agitated—to the point of making a scene. So, we left promptly after that.

When we got home, Katie ran into the house and down the hallway. Rob went back to check on her not long after and discovered Katie had cut her arm so badly that she needed to go to the

ER to get stitches. It looked bad, but her goal hadn't been to kill herself, and she absolutely hadn't intended to cut so deep. She had just gotten angry and upset and reacted by using a negative coping skill.

Rob was very comforting and understanding toward Katie. On the other hand, I was completely angry and let her know that. It seemed like she had used cutting to get back at me more than anything. And now we had to pay for a trip to the ER as well. All in all, what had started as a pleasant evening had turned out to be yet another intense and dramatic night in our household.

LAUREN

Spring 2017

Katie and I pushed through the colorful front doors and made our way to the hostess station.

"Two?" inquired the black-haired girl standing behind the wooden lectern.

"Yes, please."

"Follow me!"

We ended up in a booth near the back of the restaurant in the vicinity of the kitchen and the bathrooms. For a moment, we settled in, pulling off our jackets and tasting some of the chips and salsa that had been placed on our table. Then, we just looked at each other for a moment.

"Soo . . . What's up?" I asked.

Katie, who had been looking a little uncomfortable, burst into laughter. I loved the sound of it—rich and deep and open. I was always happiest when Katie was in a good place, and she was in a good place that night.

"Not much, dude. How about you?"

"Same."

We lapsed into silence again.

"Can I take your order?" The smiling waiter had a sharp Mexican accent and a notebook at the ready.

"Uh, yeah. I'll have a bean dip and a margarita—frozen with salt. What are you getting, Katie?"

"I'm gonna get the quesadilla Jalisco. Can I also get some rice on the side?"

"Yeah, sure."

"Thank you."

Before we could descend into awkwardness again, I spoke. "Man, I'm excited for that margarita. It's been a rough week at work so far."

"What's been going on?"

"Well . . ."

Just like that, the conversation was flowing. Katie and I have always been completely different, so we have a hard time communicating. We have different styles, needs, and expectations, so our intended messages are often misinterpreted or skewed. But Katie is my sister, and I always treasure my quality time with her. I was glad we'd been able to grab dinner for the first time in a long time.

A couple of months later, we would be back at El Maguey celebrating her twenty-first birthday, drinking margaritas and being silly together. I would be teaching her how to take a tequila shot and taking pictures of her downing it while laughing at her puckered-up face. We would be happy and carefree and together. Though there would be countless more dips in our relationship, from that night on, our sisterhood would gradually improve, becoming deeper and sweeter.

"Katie, I think our waiter has a crush on you," I giggled, sipping on my margarita and raising my eyebrows suggestively.

"What? No, I don't think so."

"He keeps looking over here! He thinks you're cute!"

"I mean, who wouldn't be interested in this?" she teased, gesturing toward herself with bravado.

"Good point," I chuckled.

"Lauren, can I ask you something kind of serious?"

I hesitated. *Oh boy*. This was why we didn't spend that much one-on-one time together. It usually led to serious conversations that almost always ended with crying and/or yelling.

"Um, sure. What's up?"

"Are you mad at me?"

"No. I mean, I'm not really happy about what happened a couple of weeks ago. I think that you didn't treat Mom fairly at all, and that was upsetting. But that doesn't mean I'm mad at you. I always love you no matter what."

"Okay, 'cause . . . I think Sarah's mad at me."

"No, she's not, Katie. I just talked to her about it a few days ago. She was also upset with you for a little while, but you know Sarah. She got over it really fast. She's not one to stay mad or hold a grudge."

"Yeah, she told me that she wasn't angry with me, but it just seems like she hasn't been talking to me lately, so I'm not sure if I believe her."

I sighed. "Katie, she's really not mad at you. She's just been super busy with school lately. You know how much she has going on."

"Okay, it's just that everyone has been walking on eggshells around me, and I hate that. I just want everyone to be normal. It really makes me mad when people aren't honest about what they really think and feel."

This time, I had to pause for a moment before responding. I had something to say, but I knew I had to say it in a way that would be meaningful to her. Otherwise, she would respond badly.

"Look, Katie. I understand that you don't want us to walk on eggshells. I understand why it would bother you that we walk on eggshells. I just . . . I think what you don't understand is how hard it is for *us*. It's just safer to walk on eggshells sometimes. None of us wants to be the person who sets you off."

"But I'm doing so amazing right now. And I just want everyone to be open with me. I need that from you."

"Katie . . . It's just . . . There've been so many times when I found myself waiting by the garage, hoping you would come back home, terrified that what I'd said or done had driven you to kill yourself. That's a lot of pressure on a person. It really takes a toll psychologically."

Katie huffed, frustrated but still pleasant. "You're just really important to me, Lauren. I want for us to have a close relationship. But right now, it doesn't seem like we do."

"I know." I frowned, looking down at my plate. "But things have been so much better between us lately. We don't talk or hang out all the time, but we also don't really fight anymore."

"Yeah." Katie paused thoughtfully. "But . . . I want to have that close relationship with you. I want for us to talk and hang out a lot more than we do."

"I want that too! I just get nervous because when we spend a lot of time together, we end up fighting. I end up upsetting you, and then I have to worry about whether you're going to hurt yourself or anything like that as a result. I think, personally, I would rather have a somewhat distant but super positive relationship than a close but strained one."

Her face scrunched up, and I instantly regretted speaking my mind—not "walking on eggshells." I had been a little too honest, and she was reacting emotionally—the opposite of what I wanted.

"But that's not fair to me. I want to have a close relationship with you. That's what's more important to me."

"I mean, I want that too, but if it's a choice between the two options, I'd rather have a positive relationship and not talk all the time." She was clearly upset now, her face red and her eyes watery.

"Katie . . ." I began exhaustedly. "This is why I walk on eggshells sometimes. All I wanted was a nice dinner with my little sister, and now it's become this big dramatic thing."

She began crying in earnest, head bowed before me, clearly distraught.

"This kind of proves my point . . ." I commented softly. I'm not sure if she heard me.

"How is everything?" Our waiter had returned. "Oh, are you all right?" he asked, turning to Katie in concern.

"Yeah, I'm fine," she responded, trying to mop up her face with her sleeve, but there were too many tears to deal with that hastily.

"What's that? Are you okay?" asked the waiter again, this time a little alarmed.

Katie glanced down and noticed that her other sleeve was pulled up to her elbow, revealing the many scars from her cutting. "Oh, that. Yes, I'm fine. Everything's all right." She quickly pulled her sleeve back down, a little caught off guard.

"Okay. Well, you just let me know if you need anything." He was looking directly at Katie when he said this. In fact, he'd been looking at her the entire conversation.

"Sounds good. Thanks."

"See! He likes you!" I hissed the second he was out of earshot. "What did I tell you!"

"Oh my gosh, I think he does! He was really worried about me."

"I know! What are you gonna do if he asks for your number?"

"Oh, I don't know. I'm sure he won't."

"Oh, yeah right. He's still looking at you from way over there! He's super into you. Maybe he'll just leave you *his* number."

Katie giggled, hiding her face a little in embarrassment, but I could tell the waiter's interest was giving her a little confidence boost. I was glad for that because she's a much more beautiful, funny, and loving person than she even realizes. She needed to be reminded of those qualities by an impartial third party.

An hour later, we walked out of El Maguey clutching our to-go boxes. It had been really rocky for several moments, but we'd been able to steer into safer waters pretty quickly.

I did have hope for our relationship, and I did want all three of us sisters to be as close as my mom and my aunts one day. But at that point, I just wanted to cherish our really good times, even if they were fewer in between. I figured everything would turn out okay eventually. And no matter what, I would be there for Katie and love her with everything I've got.

"Good night, Katie. Get home safe."

"I will. Thanks for getting dinner with me!"

"You're welcome," I smiled. "Bye."

I hopped into my car and steered to the stoplight, reflecting on the evening. Things weren't perfect, but for the moment, they were pretty darn good.

MOM

Spring 2017

Katie had made friends with one of the staff members at the hospital. Every year, that staff member organized a Suicide Prevention Workshop. She had even invited Katie to speak the following year as long as she attended the workshop this year to learn more about it.

Katie asked if I would take off work that day and attend the workshop with her. Rob and I were not happy that someone had offered this to Katie when she was not in a healthy place, so I hadn't wanted her to go at all. But she insisted she would attend no matter what, so I figured that I would at least like to be there with her.

When the day came, we got up early; drove through Starbucks, of course; and got to the church where the workshop was being held with plenty of time to spare. The room was filling up quickly. Katie and I sat quietly, not sure what to expect.

It began with the organizer sharing her personal experience. Her brother had died by suicide when they were younger, and it had left a significant impact on her life. That was followed by more stories and discussions by professionals who inspired hope.

Katie had not been in recovery for very long at this point, and it was difficult for her to listen to everything that was being said. She was visibly distraught throughout much of the day. In fact, she pretty much just sat there and cried the whole time because it was so hard for her to hear all these emotionally charged stories. It was really triggering for someone who was so early in her recovery.

I totally regretted letting Katie attend the workshop. She ended up back at the hospital not long after that, and she didn't end up speaking at the workshop the following year. It was just too much.

MOM

Spring 2017

The weather outside perfectly matched my mood. It was rainy and dreary, though it finally felt like spring. It had been a very long and tiring few weeks.

Three weeks prior, my phone had rung at 4:05 in the afternoon.

"Hello," I answered.

"Hi, Anne. This is Michelle from Mercy Jefferson."

My heart sank. Michelle was the therapist Katie had become very close with when she was inpatient at that facility. We hadn't heard from her in several months.

"I wanted to let you know that Katie reached out to me today to ask if she could meet with me for just ten minutes. I told her that I couldn't because I had a wake to go to and asked her if everything was okay. Katie told me that everything was fine, but she wanted me to know that I was a good therapist. She was sure to tell me that what I do matters and I truly help people."

"It sounds like she was saying goodbye to you," I remarked in alarm.

"Yes, that's what I thought too. I just wanted you to be aware so you could keep an eye on her."

I drove home, preoccupied by concerns about Katie. She had clearly not been doing great over the previous few weeks, but this really seemed to be coming out of the blue to me.

When I arrived home, I saw that Katie's car was gone. "Where's Katie?" I asked Rob, trying not to sound too freaked out.

"She said she was going up to Target."

That concerned me because the last time she was in the hospital, she had taken several Ibuprofens. The doctors had told her (foolishly, in my opinion) that she was lucky she had taken that and not Tylenol. If she'd taken Tylenol, she would have been sent to the ICU, as she would have been in danger of having her organs shut down. What if she'd gone to Target to buy Tylenol?

About fifteen minutes later, Katie came home with a Target bag.

"What'd you buy?" I asked.

"Just gum."

I didn't trust that she was telling me the truth, so I went back to Katie's room to talk to her. She was lying on her bed crying.

"What's going on?" I asked.

"Nothing."

"Clearly something is going on. Do you think you need to go to the hospital?"

"No! I'm never going to the hospital again! What's the point? I go, I get better, but it always gets bad again. I can't do this anymore. I'm just so tired."

I kept her company for about fifteen minutes and then went into the family room. I had just sat down when my phone rang again. This time, it was Charisse from church.

"Anne, this is Charisse. I just got a very strange text from Katie, and I'm extremely concerned." She read the text to me, and I instantly knew that Katie was also saying goodbye to her.

"She's refusing to go to the hospital," I told her desperately.

"Oh no. I'll call Katie and try to convince her to go."

A little while later, Katie came out of her room with her phone to her ear. When I heard her tell Charisse that she would go to inpatient, I immediately went to Katie's room and began packing a small bag.

Rob stayed home with Sarah, and I drove Katie to the Mercy St. Louis ER. When we arrived, it was a complete madhouse! There were people *everywhere*. It was already 7:00 p.m., so I knew it was going to be a long night.

Katie cried the whole time and said she just didn't want to be there. That was very different from how things had been in the past. Usually, she was okay with going to the ER because she knew she needed help. In this moment, she seemed completely drained of hope.

We took a seat in the waiting room and waited for them to call her name. About a half hour later, they called for "Katie." We went into the triage area where the nurses took her vitals and asked lots of questions. Unfortunately, this was all too familiar to me!

We were only in there about five minutes, and then we were back in the waiting room. At this point, we were both starving. I called Rob to see if he would bring us McDonald's. Thankfully, we were able to get some food in us since they didn't take her back to a room until after 9:00 p.m.

When you go to the emergency room for this sort of thing, there's a certain protocol. First, you have to get completely undressed and put on paper scrubs and hospital-issued no-slide socks. The next step is to put all your belongings into a bag. You have to give up your phone as well. Katie knew the routine, so she readily complied.

The ER also requires blood work and a urine sample so they can see if you have any drugs in your system. I asked Katie several times if she had taken anything, and she told me no. But again, I just didn't trust that she was telling me the truth.

In the past, when Katie attempted suicide, it seemed like she was really just acting out to get help. For example, we would look at her search history and see that she had Googled how many pills were required to actually kill her . . . and then she would take just a little less than that during her suicide attempt. So, we believed she didn't truly want to kill herself in those moments—she just didn't know what else to do, especially with the suicidal urges she was experiencing. In all honesty, our biggest concern was that she would *accidentally* kill herself during these almost suicide attempts. But now, for the first time, I really felt like she wanted to end her life. To stop the pain permanently.

The doctor was very young but businesslike. When she walked in, she asked me to step out of the room so she could talk to Katie. About ten minutes later, she came out to speak with me.

"We'll definitely be keeping her. Do you know what Katie's plan was?"

"I knew she had a plan, but I didn't know what the plan was specifically. Did she tell you?"

"Yes. She intended to take all her Wellbutrin. She had enough pills to complete the action. Does Katie have access to her medications, or do you keep them locked up somewhere?"

"I . . . Katie has her medications. She—she's almost twenty-one years old . . . She needs to be responsible for that." Talk about feeling like a crappy mom! I don't think the doctor was passing judgment, but it sure made me feel bad.

Once I knew Katie was going to be admitted, I felt comfortable going home. I knew it would be a while before she would be transported to the behavioral health area. Little did I know how long and winding this newest journey was going to be!

LAUREN

Spring 2017

Pain has always caused me to experience the world differently. When I'm suffering from immense emotional damage,
everything around me seems to shimmer, then come brightly into
focus. I feel more alive than ever, but it's not a good feeling. It's . . .
overwhelming. Like I can't escape the harsh vibrance of everyone
and everything around me.

The day after Katie planned to commit suicide (again), I
drifted through time and space, hazy from the world's assault on
my senses. My surroundings rushed at me, screamed at me, but I
remained silent.

I haven't cried yet.

Everything was so vivid, so sharp. My skin, my eardrums, my
eyeballs prickled and twitched as if the very air was clawing at
them. It was a miserable, lonely, maddening sensation. As I sat at
work, trying to concentrate on my everyday tasks—even though
this did not seem like an everyday day—I put my fingers to my
temples and rubbed hard. I'd been quieter than usual, and my

motivation had been sporadic, but I'd managed to keep it together without my coworkers realizing crazy things were happening in my family.

I haven't cried yet.

As I drove home, the trees and cars and lights seemed brighter than ever. I could barely stand to look anywhere, my eyes worn and uncaring.

Why would I want to feel so alive? My sister was almost dead. She could have been dead. And the more often she tried to kill herself, the more sure I was that she really would do it. My eyes burned as I helplessly imagined what I would do if she was gone. No tears fell.

I haven't cried yet.

SARAH

Spring 2017

With everything going on with Katie—her being in the hospital for weeks and me not being old enough to visit her—I felt emotionally strained. But I still had to go to school every day and live my life like normal. The school counselors weren't much help because they only knew how to deal with academic issues, but luckily, there was an emotional counselor available for me to talk to. Unluckily, the emotional counselor wasn't *regularly* available.

I thought it was a huge issue that our school didn't have enough money and resources to provide an emotional counselor all the time. Almost everyone you talk to has been affected by some sort of mental health issue, whether it's depression, anxiety, or something else. I've found that, especially in high school, there are so many kids affected by it. I feel like it's just growing, and every kid needs that support, whether it's them dealing with a mental health issue or a family member or friend.

Sometimes, all the weight of sadness and anxiety can be too much. Even if it's somebody else and you feel like you have to be there for them, that can put a huge weight on you. You can't always deal with that on your own, and it's important to have a system in high school to ensure there is someone there for these kids to lean on.

The fact that our school's emotional counselor was only there two and a half days a week and there was so much need for them that they had to turn people away . . . It just sucked. I was glad that I got to talk to the emotional counselor, but when I did talk to her, I knew there were other kids who couldn't meet with her. It made me feel almost guilty. And if there was a day when I needed to talk to her, but she already had kids who were scheduled to meet with her, then I didn't get to. That's just how her time was spent. How do you prioritize which kid you're gonna see that day? Which kid's struggling the most? How do you determine that? It was just hard.

Mom actually sent an email trying to explain the importance of the support system for every kid. To our dismay, the school said they understood but indicated they wouldn't do anything about it. It was like, "We care about our students, but only a little bit."

I've been out of high school for several years now, so I don't know what changes might have been applied since I graduated. I can only hope that my high school has recognized the importance of mental health support with more than just empty words.

MOM

Summer 2017

After her foiled plan to commit suicide, Katie remained at the hospital for a record seven weeks. While there, she was diagnosed with treatment-resistant depression, which was, obviously, very discouraging for all of us.

At that point, Dr. Bradenton recommended that she have ECT (otherwise known as electric convulsive therapy). This is basically modern-day electric shock therapy, and it's said to be useful for especially stubborn cases of mental illness.

Rob and I were both very hesitant! We were terrified of what would happen if ECT failed because it felt like Katie was putting all her eggs in one basket. It seemed like her last-ditch effort, and we worried that if it didn't work, it would make her feel more helpless than ever.

Plus, ECT just sounded like a risky thing. So, we weren't thrilled with the idea. But the hospital had us come in to watch an informational video and told us that it was nothing like it was years ago. They were able to control the seizures that ECT brought on, and it only lasted a few minutes. The only side effect was that she could have some memory loss.

At Katie's insistence, we decided to take the attitude that it was worth trying since nothing else seemed to be working. She had a total of eight treatments over the course of a couple of weeks. We waited anxiously to see if the ECT would help.

While she was at the hospital, I asked the psychiatrist who was in charge of her ECT treatments, "What is your opinion of what's going on with Katie? What would your diagnosis be?" I just wanted to get a different perspective.

He said she clearly exhibited some signs of borderline personality disorder, which threw me a little bit even though I had gotten this impression from other doctors before. The psychiatrist recommended a relevant book for me to check out, so I immediately bought it to see what I thought.

A few weeks later, Katie and I met with her therapist. Katie went back to talk first, and when Kelli came out to get me, I quietly asked her if she thought Katie had borderline personality disorder. (I didn't want Katie to hear me asking because I knew it was upsetting to her.) Kelli nodded her head yes.

However, Dr. Bradenton disagreed, maintaining, "She absolutely does not have borderline personality disorder. You need to have five of the criteria in order to get that diagnosis, and she absolutely does not meet five of the criteria."

So, the interesting takeaway here is that, unfortunately, there's not a blood test. There's not an imaging machine you can put people in to get some diagnosis that's definitive. It's all subjective, and you just have to learn what you can about all of it.

On that note, you should share as much as you can with the doctors because they're only able to diagnose and help based on all the information they have. So, it's super important to communicate, communicate, communicate. Even when your child comes of age, and the doctors can no longer share things with you (which becomes very frustrating), that doesn't mean you can't share things with them. You can always talk to them and offer your insights—they just won't give you information back. If you see a doctor who won't let you talk to them and give them information, you probably should find a new doctor.

Eventually, Katie was released to come back home. She was agitated and upset about leaving because she felt she wasn't ready, but she had been gone for so long that we hoped being home would prove a positive change. Unfortunately, while it had been stressful to go for her visiting hour at 6:00 p.m. every day, and while we were glad to have her with us again, her being home presented a whole different set of challenges for us.

Katie was by no means better. Though ECT typically works right away, that wasn't the case for Katie. In fact, it didn't seem to work for her at all. Still, she experienced the side effects and had some memory loss for a while. Luckily, over time, the memory loss seemed to get better. Unluckily, her mental state did not.

SARAH

Fall 2017

I walked through the door, hoping to be greeted by Katie, who had just been discharged from the hospital after being gone for weeks. Unfortunately, I was merely greeted by the lonely barks of the dogs. My head buzzing with quiet worry, I sat in the tattered armchair in front of the TV, staring blankly toward the door. My heartbeat sped up steadily as I became increasingly anxious.

Suddenly, I heard the garage door open, and the dogs started howling again, jumping up and down in a frenzy. I stood, starting for the kitchen as the door opened. Though I expected to see a smile across Katie's face, all I saw was frustration.

"What's wrong?" I asked, giving her a careful hug.

"Nothing," she replied without emotion. "I'm fine."

Thinking she needed some space, I returned to the chair and began mindlessly playing on my phone. Sometime later, I was abruptly snapped out of a reverie as I heard the garage door shutting once more. *Katie's probably just getting the rest of her clothes from the car*, I thought to myself, not feeling particularly worried. I turned my attention back to my phone, but moments later, I was interrupted by my dad.

"Where did she go?" He sounded panicked.

"I don't know. I didn't know she left," I responded, feeling defensive.

My dad became frustrated and worried, not knowing where she'd run off to. However, a few minutes later, she returned home with food from Culver's. Silent relief filled the air; we instantly felt better just knowing she was safe.

Hoping to stay out of everyone's way, I withdrew from the common area of the house to spend some time in my room. As Katie walked to her room, she poked her head into the doorway of mine and asked if I wanted to hang with her. So, I followed her into her sanctuary and started playing with our dogs as I tried to make conversation to lighten the mood.

At first, I thought it was working, but I was soon thrown off guard when Katie asked, "Do you know what they did?"

"No, what did they do?" I responded, thinking we were still talking about the dogs, our previous topic of conversation.

"When I was supposed to be discharged from the hospital, the nurses told me that I can't go to IOP for another week. I told them I'd only feel safe leaving the hospital if I'd have something to do every day rather than sit in my room, staring at the walls and becoming more depressed. I refused to sign the discharge papers, so they called Mom and Dad, telling them I was ready to leave. Then, Dad showed up and I was really mad because I wasn't ready to go. I had to rush and sign the papers and then get all of my clothes put together, and now I'm not even sure if I should have left the hospital."

"Did you tell Mom or Dad?"

"No. They don't care. Dad's a guy—he doesn't understand. He doesn't care about me."

"That's not true! Why do you always think people don't care about you? We're your family. We'll always love and support you."

She began to cry as she spat out, "No, I'm a burden. I have ruined your lives, and you don't want to deal with me anymore. It would be better if I was just gone."

Try as I might to convince Katie that she is cared about and loved by many, it just wasn't getting through to her. I asked if I could go tell Dad what was going on, and at first, she said yes. However, as I began to leave the room, she started crying harder.

"I'm fine," she insisted. "I don't need Dad."

Nonetheless, I ran down the hall and into my dad's office to tell him that things weren't okay Immediately, he raced to her room to comfort her as I rushed back to my own room, tears rolling hotly down my cheeks.

I called my mom to tell her she needed to come home because Katie was having a breakdown. She told me that she would leave work right away and everything would be all right. As soon as I got off the phone with her, I lay down on my bed. All my fear and sadness rose from my stomach, making me feel sick, and I began sobbing uncontrollably. Despite the rush of emotions coursing through my body, I tried to stay quiet so that Katie couldn't hear me in the next room.

Suddenly determined to escape from the chaos, I called my oldest sister, Lauren, hoping I could find a place to go for the night. She didn't answer her phone, so I left a voicemail and text message. Then, I frantically texted Lauren's boyfriend, Jordan, to ask whether he was with Lauren or knew where she was.

I just got off work and I'm not sure where Lauren is, but I'll try to get ahold of her. What's wrong? Can I help with anything? he responded.

I sat up and perched on the edge of my bed, staring at the screen of my phone as tears fell down my face, waiting for something—anything—to happen. Finally, after what felt like hours but was really fewer than ten minutes, Lauren called me back. In a panic, I tried to explain what had happened and asked if I could spend the night at her apartment so I wouldn't have to hear Katie's turmoil all night.

"I can come pick you up, and we can drive around for a little while, but I have plans tonight, so if you go to my apartment, you'll be there by yourself."

After some deliberation, I decided to drive around with her and then come back home. She picked me up a few minutes later, and we drove in circles around the neighborhood, talking about everything Katie had told me. After about ten minutes of throwing up my feelings to her, I finally calmed down, and Lauren drove me back home.

"I love you," said Lauren before I got out of the car. "Call me if you need anything else."

"Okay. Thanks, Lauren."

I got out of her car and walked slowly around the back of the house to the open garage. I stopped at the door to the kitchen and took a deep breath, trying to gather the strength to open the door and walk into my own nightmare.

In the few seconds it took for me to brace myself, I thought of all the horrible possibilities of what could be happening just beyond the door. She could be gone, already back at the hospital. She could be telling my parents all the disturbing thoughts running through her head. The worst possibility of all crept into the back of my mind: she could be dead. I pushed it away before fully processing it, knowing it would be too much for me to handle. I quickly went inside where I was ambushed by worried parents.

"Where were you?" my dad demanded.

"Are you okay?" my mom shouted down the hall as she walked from Katie's bedroom to the family room.

"Yeah. I'm fine. I just drove around with Lauren for a few minutes. I'm sorry I didn't say anything, Dad. I didn't want to bother you while you were talking to Katie." My voice was dim and dull.

"It's okay. Are you hungry? We can go get some dinner if you want," my dad asked, and I knew he was trying to get me out of the house.

We decided to go to Circle 7 Ranch and order some burgers. The wait was long, and there was no parking, so we were able to escape from the house for a long time. I was quiet at first, but about fifteen minutes in, my dad got me talking, and for a few minutes, I forgot about all the stuff waiting for me at home. For a moment, I was happy.

My dad and I don't do things together very often, but that night, I saw a whole new part of him. He was able to put a bright smile on my face on a night when I just wanted to crawl up in a ball and cry. For that, I am thankful.

The rest of the night was mostly calm, and I went to sleep praying for a better day tomorrow.

LAUREN

Fall 2017

Jordan and I had been living together for one month. It was a pretty significant adjustment, going from seeing each other three or so times a week to sharing a living space, but things were going well (even though I had to badger Jordan to do the dang dishes).

Our new home was a lovely townhouse located near Grant's Farm. We didn't have a ton of spare money, but we'd decorated our new living space as elegantly as we could given our limited resources. We absolutely loved it. It was *ours*.

Shortly before the move, we had committed to adopting a red merle Australian shepherd. (Okay, I committed, and Jordan half-heartedly agreed.) We had finally picked her up that Saturday, and she was gorgeous and tiny and so cute. We instantly loved her! Even Jordan couldn't stop holding her and kissing her. For the first time probably ever, Jordan and I wholeheartedly agreed on something, deciding to name her Harper Lee after the author of *To Kill a Mockingbird*. I hoped our little girl would live up to her strong name.

Even though we'd been moved in for a month, no one had really seen our new place. It had taken a little while to get everything perfectly in order, and we had known everyone would just want to come over again later anyway to meet our new pup. So, the Sunday after we picked up teeny Harper, we had a puppy-shower-slash-housewarming party.

That morning, I found myself frantically zipping around the kitchen, cooking several things at once. We were planning on having around forty people come by, so we needed plenty of food. Unfortunately, I had only started seriously learning how to cook when Jordan and I first moved in together, so I was still very much a novice. Whatever the estimated preparation time was, I unfailingly managed to take twice as long—at a minimum. So, unsurprisingly, my stress levels were through the roof.

My family was supposed to come early to help get everything ready. As usual, they arrived later than intended, only ten or fifteen minutes before everyone else. My nerves were already stretched to the breaking point, so I was a little snappy and short. I felt like I still had a million things to do before our guests arrived.

Katie, who had only recently been released from the hospital after staying there for what felt like *forever*, shuffled into the kitchen where I was still flying from counter to stove to table. She smiled slightly and lifted her arms up, her eyebrows lifting hopefully. "Can I get a hug?" she asked.

"Not right now. I'm very busy," I barked, carrying a hot dish of buffalo chicken dip to the table and glancing around for a bowl to put the tortilla chips in.

Katie's face fell, and she brushed out of the room with her head lowered. I felt a giant twinge of guilt but didn't have time to find Katie and apologize. Besides, she knew I wasn't a big fan of hugs. Clearly, now wasn't the time.

Moments later, a steady stream of friends and family filtered into the townhouse, congregating in the living room and kitchen, eventually spilling onto the back patio as space became limited. Hosting and greeting newcomers kept me occupied for a little while, but as soon as I had the chance, I found my mom and asked where Katie was.

"She left a while ago. She was only here for a few minutes."

"I kind of snapped at her . . ."

"Yeah," sighed my mom. "Would it be okay if we left here in a minute? It's getting a little too crowded anyway."

"Sure," I replied, trying not to sound upset. Internally, I fixated on the fact that my own immediate family was the first to leave the party—by a long shot. My mom might have said it was to accommodate the swelling crowd of partygoers, but I knew it was because of Katie. As usual.

At the same time, I was beating myself up, silently chastising myself for letting my stress drive my actions. Katie had just gotten discharged from the hospital. I should have run to her, wrapped her in a hug, told her how glad I was she was home. I should have swallowed my aggravation, my exhaustion with Katie's never-ending mental health challenges, and been the loving big sister. But I'd failed.

My family left, and I was kept busy by the guests filtering in and out. I was enjoying myself, but whenever I wasn't refilling chip bowls, handing out beers, or chatting with people, my mind automatically turned to Katie. I felt a deep sense of foreboding.

Something bad is going to happen . . .

And it's going to be my fault.

Jordan, without looking at me, grabbed my hand and squeezed. I closed my eyes and breathed.

MOM

Fall 2017

I knew that Katie wasn't doing very well (and maybe shouldn't have been released from the hospital), but she was starting IOP that day, so I knew she'd be somewhere safe. I had a meeting about two hours away with one of my brokers, so I couldn't keep an eye on her. It made me a little worried, but there wasn't much I could do.

"Are you okay?" I asked Katie before I left.

"Yeah . . . Just a bit uneasy."

"You'd better not do anything!"

"I won't."

"Good." Feeling a tad reassured, I left home and went to pick up my broker.

I had an app on my phone that let me see where Katie was. I knew that she would need to go through intake before starting IOP, so when I looked at my phone at about 10:00 a.m. and saw that she was at Mercy Hospital, I thought maybe that's why she was there. (Mercy's IOP is usually located off the hospital's main campus, so that's why I was confused.)

Still feeling a little unsettled, I sent Rob a text before I went in to get my broker. We both agreed that everything was probably fine, and I tried to put it from my mind and focus on my job.

After our meeting, I dropped my broker off at her office and checked my phone again to see where Katie was. It still showed she was at Mercy. At this point, I was beginning to get more concerned, but I started my way back to St. Louis thinking I could deal with it when I got home.

At about 2:30 p.m., when I could see that Katie was still at Mercy, I called her, but she didn't answer. Then, I left a message at the doctor's office to ask if they had moved IOP to Mercy Hospital.

About twenty minutes later, I received a call from the doctor's office saying they were so sorry! They were very surprised that no one had called me. Before going into IOP that morning, Katie had taken thirty-two pills in her car. She had even written notes for everyone. At some point, she'd started to feel really sick, and it had freaked her out, so she'd gone into the building. It was then that she'd told them what she'd done and fallen down on the floor. They'd immediately called 911, and she'd been transported to Mercy ER.

My initial reaction was anger—anger driven by fear. Fear that she could have actually died. Fear that I could have gotten a phone call saying she was gone forever. Fear that I could be planning a funeral right now. And . . . anger that she'd done this.

I got home and told Rob what had happened. Then, I went to Mercy to check on Katie. I was so furious that when I saw her, I told her I was extremely angry and wasn't going to stay with her in the ER. I'd just wanted to come up and make sure she was okay. Then, I left and went home. Heartbroken.

They admitted Katie to the medical psychiatric unit, and this is where she stayed for another several weeks. We did go up and see her every day for visiting hours: 6:00 to 7:00 p.m. Some days, the visits were good, and the conversations went well. Other days were difficult with not much discussion.

At some point, I told Katie that the definition of insanity was to do the same thing over and over again and expect a different result. I thought it was time to do something different. So, I spoke with Kelli, Katie's therapist, and she recommended a residential facility up near Chicago called Timberline Knolls. Katie's psychiatrist agreed that it was a good idea to try a residential facility, which further bolstered our confidence in this new direction.

It was time to do some research again. The reviews for Timberline Knolls were not the best. In fact, they were downright horrible! But I also knew that the residents of facilities like these may not usually have the most positive response, and the reviews were mostly from residents. So, I didn't dismiss it outright as a bad option.

I was feeling very drawn to the place for many reasons. One, it took our insurance (that was huge). Two, it was only five hours away (not far compared to other options). And three, it was recommended by Katie's therapist. That certainly counted for something.

To our relief, Katie agreed that this was a good next step. I also told Katie that I thought she needed a new therapist when she came back home. I liked Kelli, but it seemed like Katie wasn't always comfortable sharing things with her. And if you can't share with your therapist, they're not going to be very effective for you. But that was a decision that would be made later once she returned home—whenever that would be.

SARAH

Fall 2017

On Sunday, my mom, Katie, and I ran a few errands and relaxed at home. I tried to stay positive about what was going on with Katie, but she acted like a robot. She seemed like she was going through the motions, but there was absolutely no emotion. She was usually sad and crying or mad and yelling, but this time, she was nothing. I could see in her eyes that she'd given up and no longer had the will to fight.

On Monday, I didn't have school, so I stayed at home getting caught up with schoolwork while binge-watching *Grey's Anatomy*. Around 10:00 a.m., my dad walked into the family room and sat down in the chair.

"Where's Katie?" I asked, unsure whether she was at IOP, at therapy, or just running errands.

"She's supposed to be at IOP, but Mom just texted me after looking at Katie's location, and it says she's at Mercy Hospital."

"Huh."

We were confused, but we came to the conclusion that she may have had to go through intake at the hospital to go to IOP. So, we went on with our day, assuming everything was going well.

In reality, Katie had attempted to take her life yet again and had spent the day at the hospital. But I was unaware of what had happened until my mom came home and told me.

As soon as she came through the door, I looked up from my laptop. She walked into the family room with tears silently falling off her chin onto her turtleneck, and I immediately embraced her in a hug. Again, frantic thoughts fluttered through my mind. I just knew something had happened to Katie.

"What's wrong?" I asked desperately, but my mom had a hard time getting the words out. My dread grew as my mom floundered, and the thought of Katie being gone lingered a little longer than it usually did in situations like this. "Please," I asked, willing Mom to find her voice.

"Katie—she overdosed this morning. Don't worry—she's okay. She's at the hospital. She's been there all day."

I had questions, but I bit my lip. I didn't want to make my mom even more upset than she already was. Luckily, a little while later, she got a phone call from Katie's therapist who was worried because Katie had missed her appointment that night. I listened in as she told the story:

Katie had come up with a plan to kill herself sometime over the weekend and, on Sunday, had left Lauren's housewarming party early to get a bottle of alcohol from the store. Then, that morning, she'd gone to IOP and, while sitting in the parking lot, taken fifteen Temazepam and seventeen Ritalin pills. She'd washed it down with a swig of alcohol, which she didn't like and ended up never drinking again.

A few minutes later, she'd stumbled into the building, where she'd fallen to the ground. When she told one of the workers there what she'd done, they'd called 911, and she'd been taken to Mercy Hospital in an ambulance. Luckily, she'd thrown up most of the medicine, so they didn't end up having to pump her stomach.

Somehow, she regretted not going through with it and still wished she would have died, even hours later once my mom had arrived to see her.

This was the umpteenth time Katie had been admitted to the hospital in that year alone. As a family, we were exhausted by this continuous rollercoaster. At first, we felt frustrated that she was compelled to do this so often, though we realized that this was the nature of mental illness. After a while, the anger faded away, and we decided something had to change this time if we wanted a different result. So, Katie and my parents decided that when she got out of the hospital, she would get a new therapist and look into going to a residential facility.

It sounded like a good plan. It was a *different* plan at least. But I was scared. Katie would be so far away. How would she handle this new tactic to get her mental illness under control?

MOM

Fall 2017

We were able to get everything coordinated and approved with Timberline Knolls, but we needed to do a door-to-door transfer. This meant we had to pick Katie up from the hospital and—that same day—admit her to the residential facility hours away.

It was 7:30 a.m. when I arrived at Mercy. I parked, walked through the lobby, and took the elevator to the fifth floor. Then, I walked along the hallway until I got to the wide, locked door and picked up the red phone on the wall.

"I'm here to pick up Katie," I stated.

"We'll be out in just a little bit."

I had waited about ten minutes when the door finally opened. I was so excited to see my Katie and give her a big, huge hug! While we made the twenty-minute drive back to our house, we planned out our day. We would go home, and Katie would pack and take a shower. Then, Katie, Rob, and I would stop by Grandma's so Katie could say goodbye to her. We also stopped at Panera to get coffee and something to eat before we started the long drive up to Timberline Knolls.

It was about 10:30 a.m. before we were able to get on the road. By about 1:00 p.m., we were all in need of a restroom break, so we stopped at a McDonald's. As I was walking back to the car, my phone rang. It was Melanie from the residential facility.

"Hello?"

"Hi! When do you think you'll be arriving?"

"Oh, we should be there by 2:30 or 3:00."

"Oh, well, do you think you could wait and come tomorrow? We actually don't have any beds available right now."

I was *furious*! "No, we *cannot* wait until tomorrow because we need to do a door-to-door transfer for insurance, and we already picked Katie up from the hospital. We're already on our way there!"

"Oh, okay . . . I'll call you back."

About a half hour later, she called again.

"Go ahead and come," she said. "We'll figure something out."

We finally arrived at the facility at 2:35 p.m. Rob went in to use the restroom while Katie remained in the back seat finishing up an email to someone. I sat looking out the window at the sparkling snow.

Suddenly, a beautiful red cardinal bird landed on the snow-covered branch of the tree right in front of me. I immediately thought of my dad, who had passed away almost three years earlier. I just knew it was him there with me that day—encouraging me and giving me strength.

Rob returned, and we all went into the administration building to begin the admission process. We loitered in the waiting area for probably forty-five minutes before they finally came and took us into a small room where the process would begin. Then, they took Katie's luggage so they could go through her stuff to inventory everything and make sure what she was bringing was allowed and safe.

By about 5:30 p.m., we were told that they still didn't have a bed available, but they would put Katie in a hotel room with some other girls who also needed to be admitted. Katie, understandably, had a complete meltdown. Making the decision to come to a residential facility was not easy, and it had taken all her courage just to get there. Now she was being told there was no bed? I was not a happy camper!

"There's no way Katie is staying in a hotel with other people," I responded flatly. "And how is this going to impact insurance since it's no longer going to be a door-to-door transfer?"

"Oh, don't worry. We'll take care of that."

Timberline Knolls booked a hotel room for us in nearby Bolingbrook. At 7:30 p.m., we headed out to get dinner, then returned to our room for the night. Keep in mind that Rob and I had planned to drop Katie off at the residential facility and then turn around and drive home. We didn't bring *anything* with us. No change of clothes, no contact solution, no medications—nothing!

Still, we tried to be positive. I really felt that Timberline Knolls would make a huge difference for Katie in spite of the mix-ups at the start. I knew she would have individual therapy sessions a few times a week, and the psychiatrist would see her weekly. Meanwhile, there would be group sessions all day long every day, and we would even have family therapy sessions with her over Skype every week. All in all, Katie would be getting near constant attention while at the residential facility, and I had to maintain my hope that it would work out. So, swallowing my frustration, I resigned myself to the change of plans.

On Friday morning, we got up early and arrived at the residential facility by 8:30. They immediately got us back to a room to continue the admission process. Even getting there that early, Rob and I weren't able to leave until 2:30 that afternoon. It had literally been twenty-four hours since we'd originally arrived!

"Now, you won't be allowed to talk to Katie for at least twenty-four hours so she can get acclimated to her new environment," a nurse reminded us as we hugged Katie goodbye.

So, you can imagine my surprise when my phone rang at about 9:00 that night, and it was Katie.

"Are you okay?" I asked immediately.

"Yes. They aren't that smart here, and when I asked if I could use the phone, they said yes."

It was good to hear her voice and know that she was okay. This was just the beginning, and we believed in our hearts that she would be *more* than okay once she was able to come home.

LAUREN

Fall 2017

Katie had left for Timberline Knolls, a residential facility near Chicago, on November 16. Ever since, our family had been drifting along, hope hot in our bellies, sadness bright in our eyes.

I didn't have as difficult of a time at first. I thought about Katie and worried about how she was doing, but since I didn't live at home anymore, her absence didn't really change my everyday life. In fact, I dealt with it quite well until Thanksgiving, the first family holiday spent without her.

At first, it was kind of nice because Grandma was there, her walker and oxygen tank in tow. It was the last holiday she would spend with us outside of her retirement home. Plus, we were able to chat with our loved ones freely without worrying about whether Katie was having a meltdown in the other room. As much as we missed Katie, there was an element of relief at play knowing she was somewhere safe, and we were able to focus solely on having a good time with family.

That relief was quickly stomped out when Katie called a little while before dinner was served. Mom passed the phone around to a few people so they could talk with her and wish her a happy Thanksgiving, but Katie was tired and sad, so she didn't want to speak with everyone. Before my mom could hang up, I reached my hand out imploringly, mouthing to let me at least talk to her.

"Katie?" I asked breathlessly the moment the phone was pressed to my ear.

"Lauren? I'm glad it's you," she sighed. "I felt so awkward talking to everyone else."

"How are you doing?"

"I'm okay." Her voice was low and melancholy, and I suddenly missed her more than ever.

"I'm sorry," I murmured. "I know it must be hard to be away from home on a holiday. We miss you so much."

"I miss you too," replied Katie, who was suddenly bawling. I could tell she had been holding it in for a while.

"Aw, it's okay, Katie. There's nothing too exciting going on over here anyway. Shh, it's all right."

I sat and listened to her weep for a while, my heart breaking piece by piece at each gut-wrenching sob. Finally, I tentatively interrupted her sounds of misery. "Katie, would you like to talk to Mom again?"

"Yes," she said thickly, and I thrust the phone back at my mom, tears in my own eyes.

"Are you okay?" whispered Sarah, who was sitting on the couch beside me. I shook my head, and she wrapped her arms around me, resting her head on top of mine.

What had started out as a reasonably pleasant holiday had totally soured, becoming at least as bad as all those other Thanksgivings spent consoling a distraught Katie. I remained quiet and somber for the rest of the evening and left promptly after pie. It wasn't the same without Katie there, after all.

LAUREN

Winter 2017

It was December, but it wasn't Christmastime. Not really.

My family's house was cheerful with candles and wreaths in every window and seasonal decorations adorning the family room and Christmas tree. Christian music sang sweetly from the stereo, rejoicing in the birth of Jesus.

I lolled pointlessly on the couch, oblivious to the brightness of the scene. It was artificial anyway. We weren't going to have a merry Christmas. Nothing was right without Katie.

We had driven around looking at Christmas lights and gone to Aunt Molly and Uncle Jim's to watch *Elf*. Katie's absence had been loud and sharp, and we'd gone home before the movie had even ended. We hadn't been able to go caroling on Main Street at all—probably for the best because that would have been dismal without Katie's booming voice joining in with mine and Sarah's. I had hoped Katie would be able to come home before Christmas so I could have my sisters over to watch a Christmas movie and eat cookies, but there was no chance of that happening. She wouldn't be at our Christmas Eve celebration with Mom's family either. Without her there, I knew that what was usually my favorite night of the whole year would turn out to be one of the worst nights of all.

And then, Christmas Day—there would be no breakfast casserole and burnt sausage croissants. There would be no taking turns opening gifts and huffing good-naturedly at the ten pictures Mom had to take each time. There would be no groans and gripes every time my turn came around and I slowly and painstakingly opened each gift without tearing the wrapping paper. There would be no forgetting about our stockings until hours later, when we would light up with joy, realizing that there were just a few more surprises in store. There would be no visiting with Dad's side of the family, then coming home to relax in front of the TV as a family.

It was so hard to go through the holidays without my little sister.

I closed my eyes. Exhaled. Prayed to God for strength—and for Katie to come home soon.

SARAH

Winter 2017

When Katie went to Timberline Knolls, I felt like I was drowning. I just wanted help. I just wanted *something*. I couldn't do it on my own. So, I turned to my faith for support.

My faith was something I struggled with a lot throughout my childhood. When I was younger, my family would go to church a lot, but I didn't usually enjoy it. As I got a little bit older, I was more comfortable because I got to sit with the adults, which improved the experience. So, I got more out of church then.

Katie was always one of my role models for my faith because, when I was younger and played softball, I couldn't go to church very often due to my weekend tournaments. But Katie would always try to go, and I looked up to her for that. She was very strong in her faith, even when she was having a hard time. I aspired to maintain the same level of dedication to my faith.

One time when she was struggling more than usual, I could see that she was turning all her anger toward God. At the time, she thought, *God hates me. God is doing this to me*. Witnessing this unfamiliar side of the sister I had always looked up to introduced new doubts for me. I began to wonder, *Oh . . . Maybe He isn't there.* I didn't know what to think.

It got better when Katie started to get more involved with church again, but it wasn't perfect. Her doubts lingered, and so did mine. Plus, I just had a different experience than Katie. I always tried to go to youth group, but I never found the same community that Katie did. That almost made me turn away from God because I didn't know where I belonged.

Once Katie went to Timberline Knolls, my emotions spun out of control, and my faith went with them. I was in a low place, both emotionally and spiritually. I would get angry sometimes. I'd try to pray—try to do all kinds of things—but I felt like I was constantly being slapped down.

While attempting to surrender to God and let Him take control, I didn't feel comfortable—I didn't feel safe. I was trying to give my pain over to God, but I wasn't getting anywhere. That made it even harder. It made me feel like I was drowning and there was nothing I could do.

Luckily, my friends at the time were very strong in their faith, and they tried to help me. I still struggled and doubted, but they lifted me up and reminded me of my faith. I was able to rise above again.

LAUREN

Winter 2017

I sighed at the lines of stubbornly red lights filling the windshield. We had left fairly early to get to the Christian music concert, but we hadn't accounted for the crazy amount of traffic.

I was steadily growing aggravated by Sarah and her friend singing loudly in the seats next to me. Jordan was sitting comfortably in the front, chatting with my mom, occasionally looking back to wink jauntily in my direction.

"Mom, I think we're gonna be late." Sarah had finally put a pause on her back seat concert.

"I know," responded my mom, her hands tense on the steering wheel. I knew she wanted to get there in time to see For King and Country play the drums. It had been, by far, the best part of the concert the year before.

Much to Mom's chagrin, the traffic didn't let up the entire way to the Scottrade Center, and we arrived twenty minutes late, completely missing "Little Drummer Boy." With her emotions already stretched to the breaking point, my mom collapsed into her seat next to Aunt Maggie, and her face crumpled into tears.

"I'm so sorry! I don't know what's wrong with me," she sobbed as my aunt hugged her and rubbed her back. "I'm bummed that we missed my favorite song, but I don't know why I'm crying about it."

"It's okay, Mom," I said quietly, gently rubbing her arm. Luckily, Sarah was wrapped up in the concert with her friend and didn't notice much of what was going on.

Eventually, we were able to relax and enjoy the concert. To my relief, Mom cheered up quickly and belted out all the songs, her voice as strong as her faith. I swayed and sang under my breath, light and loving in gratitude and praise, until a powerful line that reminded me of Katie sucker punched me in the stomach. In an instant, I felt my eyes grow wet.

"Here." My mom handed me a tissue, and I looked up, smiling at her.

"You came prepared, huh?"

"Yeah," she laughed, showing me the full pack of tissues she had in her purse. "I hope I have enough for the both of us!"

By intermission, we were all in fairly good spirits. It's hard not to feel hopeful and warm when surrounded by thousands of Christians, all united in worship. Sarah and her friend twittered beside me and Jordan as we chatted happily, barely noticing as my mom turned away from us and discreetly answered her buzzing cell phone.

I broke off midsentence at my mom's suddenly strained tone; she was clearly distraught but trying to sound calm and unaffected. Her voice grew extra quiet, but I still felt the tension emanating from her body sitting so close to mine. I turned toward her and tried to guess what had happened from only one side of the conversation, but it was impossible to tell. All I knew was that something really bad had occurred. A panicked vision of Katie, peaceful and motionless in a coffin, flashed through my mind. My hand shook as I grabbed Jordan's knee.

"What happened?" I demanded as soon as my mom ended the call. The second act was just beginning to play.

"Katie's at the hospital . . ."

"*What happened*?" I repeated urgently.

"I couldn't hear her very well, but I guess she tried to kill herself. They had to take her to the hospital, and now she's staying in the behavioral health unit." As she spoke, she began crying in earnest, and my aunt pulled her over and let her sob into her shoulder.

For a long time, I wasn't able to move. The news had struck me still and silent, and I stared unseeingly ahead of me, oblivious to the music blaring throughout the stadium.

Jordan, who'd been joking around with Sarah, turned back to me and noticed my set jaw. "What's wrong?"

I gulped a few times, compelling my voice to turn back on. "Don't—don't tell Sarah. I don't want to ruin her night. Um . . . Katie just—just tried to kill herself."

Jordan put his arm around me, wordlessly supporting me as I lapsed back into silence. I was trying so hard not to cry, trying so hard to process what Katie had done. I had thought she would be safe at Timberline Knolls, thought that she wouldn't have the resources or the freedom to harm herself in any way. All of a sudden, I realized that if she was truly determined, Katie could find a way to end it. She could find a way to shred my family into a miserable pile of broken hope.

Near the end of the concert, the lead singer of Casting Crowns told a story, one of overcoming the most horrific hardships and being lifted up by the grace of God. I no longer remember the details of the personal anecdote, but in that moment, it reminded me so much of God's role in Katie's story that my heart physically hurt. As strong as I had been all night, I found I couldn't hold myself together anymore, and I broke down, sobbing unrestrainedly into my sleeves.

My sweet mom realized I was splintering, and she pulled me into her, resting her chin on my head. Instead of trying to stay stoic and strong, she cried with me, making me feel a little less sad and alone. Jordan, who was still holding my hand, squeezed hard, reminding me that he was there for me too.

Finally, I calmed down, clutching one of the tissues from my mom's purse.

"It's gonna be okay," stated my mom, sounding surprisingly self-assured. In spite of everything, she wore a small smile. Her hope kindled my hope, just barely penetrating the pain rushing through me.

I knew we had a long way to go—longer than we had hoped now that Katie was at the residential psychiatric facility—but we couldn't lose faith. God had rescued Katie and the rest of us time and time again, and He would continue to hold our family in His mighty palms.

MOM

Winter 2017

It was a pretty sad Christmas season without Katie around, but Sarah, Lauren, Jordan, my sister Maggie, and I tried to keep up some festive cheer by going to a Christian music concert in early December.

During the break between For King and Country and Casting Crowns, my phone rang. It was Katie. It was loud in the arena, so I couldn't hear very well. I just heard, "This is Katie," and then, "socks," "hospital," and "I'm fine."

"Dad's home," I responded, my voice raised in response to the noise around me. "Can you call him? I'm sorry, I just can't hear what you're saying very well." But I knew what had happened in general. She had tried to kill herself again.

Around midnight, I pulled into the driveway to my house and decided to call the nurse at Timberline Knolls just to check up on everything.

"I feel so bad telling you this," said the nurse kindly, "but Katie attempted suicide earlier this evening. She took some socks and tied them together, then put them around her neck. When her roommate found her, she was already turning blue."

"Oh my God. Is she okay?"

"We were able to get the socks off, and she could answer basic questions, but we called 911, and she's at the hospital now."

"Okay . . . Thank you for letting me know."

I generally don't have too many pity parties, but I cried myself to sleep. After I woke up on Saturday morning, I sat on the sofa all day, crying on and off. I didn't even shower or change out of my pajamas. I just let my misery and helplessness take over.

When Sunday arrived, I knew I needed to get back to life and get my errands run, but I was still really sad, thinking about what would have happened if Katie's roommate hadn't walked in when she did. Would I have been arranging for her body to be transported back home so we could have her funeral?

Overall, you could say it was a rough weekend.

SARAH

In high school, I tried to depend on myself to get through tough times rather than rely on other people. That was particularly challenging when serious things were happening, and I struggled to keep my own mental health in a good place.

I tried journaling, but this coping skill didn't click with me because I don't like to write, and my hand would get tired. Talking was helpful. Sometimes, I'd sit in my room, and if I was angry about something, I would talk out loud even if no one was there. I'd just get it out. If I was sad, I'd let myself cry. If I felt like I needed something more than that, I'd confide in Mom or Dad— usually Mom because I can connect with her better as a girl.

I remember when I learned that Katie had attempted to commit suicide while at Timberline Knolls, I was extremely upset and thought, *I really don't want to feel this way.* I needed to escape the pervasive despair that had captured my heart.

To get my mind off my sadness, Mom took me on a car ride around the fancy neighborhoods so I could "see how the rich lived" (as my grandma always jokingly said). We drove around until I had rediscovered my sense of calm. This also made an impact on my frame of mind because that's usually what my mom did with Katie. In those cases, it was always: *Katie's having a hard time . . . Drop everything and take her on a car ride to cheer her up*. On this one occasion, it was me who needed individualized attention and a distraction from my negative thoughts, and Mom gave that to me. Her offer to take me on a drive really helped and meant a lot to me too.

I also found solace in music. When I was in high school, Christian music helped me get through the hard times. But it wasn't always easy.

When Katie was struggling or in the hospital or when I was just having a hard day myself, I felt like I was in a deep hole of, *This isn't real. He doesn't care about me. I don't know why I listen to this music*. There were plenty of times when I would listen to what was once a favorite song and get angry. *This is what the music says, but that's not how it goes for me*, I'd think.

But then, other times, I'd listen to the music and believe, *That may not be happening for me in this moment, but I know that there's something more powerful going on here*. Especially when Katie was doing well, I would hear worship music on the radio and think, *He's there—He's listening*. I'd have moments when it would touch my heart, amplifying my faith.

Clearly, my relationship with God was significantly affected by my family's never-ending mental health rollercoaster. But regardless of how I was feeling in the moment, Christian music helped me recognize and face my highs and lows.

I also had a teacher who was really encouraging. One day, I went into class, and it was clear I was seriously struggling. It had obviously been a rough couple of months with Katie, and I needed to tell some teachers because I was having a hard time with my schoolwork. It felt impossible to get everything done with the chaos I was dealing with outside of school.

I was really worried about telling my teachers—worried that they weren't going to care. But when I told my math teacher, she took me into her classroom, and we had a conversation. I probably got there at 7:00 a.m. to talk to her, and we spoke all the way until school started at 7:30.

"What do you need? What's going on?" she asked.

So, I told her my family's story, and she opened up about her own history with mental health challenges. She became someone I could connect with through our stories. Whenever anything bad had happened the night before, I could go in and just talk to her about it. That brought me great comfort and helped me feel less alone when I was in the school environment.

Even though it's hard to deal with all the things that go on with Katie and her mental illness, I have gained the strength to help myself through it. Between listening to music and talking about my feelings and struggles, I have some healthy coping skills I can rely on, and I have a pretty good support system too. I guess that's all I can ask for in the situation my family is in.

LAUREN

Winter 2017

I groggily pulled on my leggings and long-sleeved T-shirt, then kissed Jordan goodbye. It was super early on Christmas morning, and he was still sleeping. As my lips left his forehead, he stirred, opening his eyes blearily.

"Are you leaving?"

"Yeah."

"Ugh it's so early!"

"I know. Sucks." I yawned and grabbed my purse, then stomped down the stairs with Harper chasing my heels. I grabbed my fluffy winter coat and headed toward the door but stopped suddenly.

"What's wrong?" asked Jordan from the top of the stairs.

"Almost forgot the cookies your mom made."

The night before, Christmas Eve, Jordan and I had brought Harper over to Jordan's parents' house. We'd opened gifts (they'd even gotten some for Harper!), munched on sweets, and watched *A Child's Christmas in Wales*. Then, before we left, Jordan's mom had pulled me aside to give me a perfectly packaged batch of homemade treats.

"This is for you and your family. I feel so bad that you're having to spend your Christmas away from home. I hope these treats will help make the day a little bit better."

"Thank you," I'd murmured, tears pricking my eyes.

Jordan's whole family had been so exceptionally kind and supportive of me since Katie had gone to Timberline Knolls. They're not usually lovey-dovey people, preferring to show their love by making fun of one another, but they had gone out of their way to express their care and concern for me during that difficult month. This showed me that they not only love me and accept me as part of their family, but that they care about my family too. As sad as I was, this compassion made room in my heart for joy and gratitude.

After I grabbed the goodies, I walked into the bright morning with Jordan by my side. When I reached my mom's car, he pulled me in and held me close. "It's gonna be okay," he said. "Text me."

"Okay," I breathed. Then, I opened the door to climb into the back. "Whoa!" Before I could move, two wriggly black dogs fell at my feet outside the car, their tongues lolling.

"Lily! Kona!" Sarah scrambled out after them, yanking on their leashes.

"Rob, help them get the dogs in the car," my mom hollered from the driver's seat. With my dad's help, we were able to wrestle the dogs into the trunk, where they whimpered and whined pathetically as everyone settled back into the car.

My mom swiftly put the car in gear and slid out of the parking spot in front of my apartment. Katie's visiting hours were from 2:00 to 5:00 p.m., so I knew we were on a timeline, and Mom was intent on getting to Timberline Knolls in plenty of time to see Katie as soon as possible.

"Can we open the middle seat yet?" asked Sarah.

"Sure. Make sure they're doing okay."

Sarah pulled the back of the seat down, and Kona immediately pushed through the small hole.

"Whoa! The hole is too big! She's getting through!" Sarah and I worked together to shove her back in and closed the gap again. "What are we gonna do? She was shaking. I think she's scared."

"Let's just crack it open," I suggested. Cautiously, I pulled on the seat just slightly, and Kona's panting snout immediately poked through. "You goof," I laughed, giving her nose a little stroke. "This'll work okay."

We were able to keep the dogs at bay for only about twenty minutes before Kona managed to muscle her way into the back seat of the car, Lily right behind her.

"It's fine," I sighed as Lily settled her sausage body onto my lap with a grunt. "I feel bad keeping them cooped up back there."

"Oh my god, they smell so bad," groaned Sarah, covering her nose with her hand. "I think one of them farted."

"Whew! Someone's stinky!" commented my dad, fanning the air in front of his face. "Was that one of the dogs?"

"Yep."

"Oh . . . I gave them each a chewy last night to keep them out of the way while I was packing some of Katie's stuff. That usually makes them pretty gassy the next day . . ."

"Mom!"

"Sorry!"

Needless to say, it was a long, cramped car ride. Finally, a little before 2:00 p.m., we made it to Timberline Knolls. I glanced around, interested but nervous. It seemed like a nice little community tucked away into the back of a suburban subdivision. There was a thick layer of snow on the ground, and white flakes were still falling by the time we arrived.

"Lauren, why don't we go sign in while Dad and Sarah wait with the dogs, and then we can switch?"

"Sounds good."

We trudged across the wet road and ducked under the cover of the overhang, then walked to the main door.

"Hi, we're here to visit Katie," said my mom, approaching the receptionist at the front desk.

"What lodge?"

"Well, she was in Willow, but now she's in Maple."

"Okay, gotcha. Here are your name tags."

"Where exactly are we going? I'm not sure where her new cabin is located . . ."

I zoned out as I noticed a man walking around outside, apparently yelling excitedly. Before my mom had finished talking to the receptionist, I slipped outside to see what was going on.

"Ashley! Ashley, sweetie! Is that you?"

"Dad?!"

"Oh, I'm so happy to see you! I'm gonna get checked in, then I'll be right there."

"All right, I know where we're going," stated my mom from right behind me, making me jump.

"Did you see that?" I asked as I followed her back to the car. "It's so sad that people have to be away from home at Christmas, but it's really kind of beautiful to see families being reunited."

"Yes. Although, honestly, Katie told me a lot of people don't get visitors. She feels really sad for them because their families won't come see them."

"That *is* really sad."

After Dad and Sarah came back with their name tags, we drove to a cabin located at the very back of the campus. We parked on the side of the road and made our way to the door, the dogs practically dragging us along.

"It's locked," I remarked, pulling on the door handle.

"Yeah, you have to ring the bell."

A few moments later, we were inside, and the charge nurse was leading us to a side room that looked like an office with a desk, random tables, and several chairs. Then, for the first time in weeks, I saw my little sister.

"Katie!" I squealed, practically jumping on her as I gave her a bear hug.

"Merry Christmas, guys!" smiled Katie as she hugged each of us. "How was the car ride?"

"Stinky."

"Can we close the door?" asked my mom. "That way, we can let the dogs off their leashes."

"No, the door has to stay open," chirped the charge nurse as she powerwalked past the room.

"That's fine."

We all sat down and secured the leashes to some of the chairs so the dogs could sort of walk around freely. For a little while, we bantered and laughed and pretended like it was a normal Christmas even though it very clearly wasn't. Then, when there was a lull in the conversation, I jumped in with what I was really curious about hearing.

"So, Katie, tell me what's been going on! How have you been doing?"

"Look . . . I don't really want to talk about how I'm doing today. It's Christmas . . . I want to talk about other stuff."

I felt an irrational surge of anger at her words. I only wanted to hear about one thing, and she was going to withhold that from me? I understood that it may not be particularly pleasant for her to talk about her mental health journey at Timberline Knolls, but I really wanted to understand what was going on—and, most importantly, when she might be coming home.

I didn't say anything, but I was annoyed. So, a few minutes later when Katie was getting testy with my dad over something silly he had said, I snapped at her a little. "Katie, it's Christmas. We don't want to talk about anything negative. Drop it."

Her face hardened, but she didn't respond, so I thought it was over. But later in the conversation, when I got heated with my dad for saying something that I believed was stereotyping people with disabilities, Katie pounced.

"Lauren, I thought we were trying not to be negative because it's Christmas."

"I was trying to defend people against an unfair judgment. *You* were just picking a fight."

"Well—"

"It's all right! Let's just all calm down," interrupted my dad.

Katie and I both slouched in our chairs, scowling at the ground. I felt sick, thinking that we had just driven all that way for me and Katie to get in a fight within the first hour of the visit.

Somehow, with my dad's help, we ended up getting the conversation going again. I was quiet for a while, feeling resentful and abashed all at once. But Katie seemed to go back to herself for the most part.

Eventually, I got up to go to the bathroom, just to get away and regroup for a moment. My mom told me that it was against the rules for the bathroom door to be closed, so I left it open. But I felt a little uneasy when I entered a stall and noticed that there were no locks. The stall doors closed, but it would be simple to push them open. So, I was quick to rejoin the group.

Around four in the afternoon, Katie left to grab some munchies for snack time. When she came back, she had her arms full of pretzels and juice.

"Here—you can have some!"

"Thanks!"

"You can throw your trash away in the garbage bin. I just have to hold on to mine so the behavioral health specialist can count and make sure I didn't take too much or not eat enough."

"They seriously, like, track what you eat?"

"Yeah."

For the rest of our visit, we played *Apples to Apples*, all too aware that our time with Katie was ticking by. Visiting hours ended at 5:00 p.m., and we felt like we needed to take advantage of every moment. Of course, eventually, our time was up.

"All right, it's time for us to leave."

I expected Katie to cry like she usually did when we visited her at the hospital at home, but she remained calm and brave.

"Okay. Thank you so much for coming to see me," she smiled, hugging everyone in turn. "I love you. Merry Christmas."

"Merry Christmas, Katie."

DAD

Winter 2017

I just want all of my girls to know how happy I am with all of you and how special this Christmas was to me. As you all know, for years now, The Crossing [our church] has emphasized that Christmas should be about far more important things than gifts and that we should focus on more relational gifting.

As we were traveling home tonight, I couldn't help but think that, for the first time, we truly reached what Greg has been preaching for the past eleven years. Had we been able to pick where and how we spent Christmas this year, I rather doubt any of us would have jumped up and down to say, "Ooh, I want to spend Christmas 2017 stuck in a car for hours on end with a couple of nasty, gas-producing canines." Likewise, I'm guessing none of us would have opted to spend Christmas Day in a mostly locked unit of a residential facility hell and gone from family and friends. While it wasn't the Christmas we might have planned, I really think it was the Christmas that each and every one of us needed!

Certainly, no one would have picked a classroom in a place almost five hours from home to celebrate, but it's not so very different from the very first Christmas in that regard. I'm guessing neither Mary nor Joseph were thinking to themselves that night, "Bonus! We get to sleep in the barn with the animals!" (I just had a mental picture of me trying to sell that to my lovely bride the night she gave birth to my Sunshine, and I can tell you, it wasn't pretty!) And as for our complaints about rawhide chewy flatulent canines, I suspect Mary and Joseph dealt with far worse from a whole array of animals that they shared their accommodations with.

Now, don't get the wrong idea about these comparisons. As wonderful and special as I find each of my daughters, I'm not suggesting any of you are the Second Coming! But today we didn't share traditional gifts wrapped in seasonal paper and ribbons. Instead, we gave of ourselves—each and every one of us—to each other. We were there for one another in a way I hadn't recognized before.

Years from now, you may look back at this Christmas as not being very much fun, but I shall remember this Christmas as our best Christmas ever!

Merry Christmas to a bunch of girls who make their father beam with pride day in and day out!

Love,
Dad

LAUREN

Winter 2018

I had a hard time after coming home from visiting Katie for Christmas. I couldn't help but feel I had ruined Christmas by getting into a disagreement with Katie. Luckily, Jordan was there to help me work through everything and get on a road to feeling better about it.

To be honest, I didn't make significant progress in coping effectively with Katie's mental illness until I started dating Jordan. As we became close and I grew to trust him more than anyone else, I was finally able to let myself feel my emotions. He provided me with a safe place to connect with my own heart and realize what was going on inside of me. I still struggle with fully giving myself over to my emotions at times, but I am so much better at acknowledging and dealing with my feelings now that I have Jordan's coaching and support.

Growing up, I felt like I had to deal with everything by myself. I didn't want to burden my parents, my sisters, or even myself with my sadness, anger, guilt, *feelings*. But . . . I wished I had someone to talk to. To cry to. To experience my emotions with me.

I remember pacing around my room, anxiety weighing on my chest like a medicine ball. I would scroll through the contacts in my cell phone, looking for someone, *anyone*, to reach out to. Every time, I would go from top to bottom without actually calling anyone. At this point, I was so emotionally damaged that I hated to bog anyone else down with my problems. So, I shoved it all aside and soldiered on.

Now that I have Jordan, I have a completely different experience. I still hesitate to express my feelings authentically with most of the people around me, even those I'm close with. In fact, one of my friends told me that when I talk about the latest dilemma with Katie, I speak as though I'm talking about someone else's life. In spite of that, I have grown much more emotionally healthy through Jordan's patient guidance. He encourages me to tell him everything, including how I feel. He tells me it's okay to cry and holds me when I do. He draws the thoughts and emotions out of me and into the sunlight. I'm learning that it's okay to feel. It doesn't make me weak. It makes me human.

I am so unbelievably grateful for Jordan—the love of my life and now my husband. Not only is he an incomparable source of joy and laughter, but he is also my comfort, my security, and my champion. He helps me be a better person and does everything he can to ensure I'm okay. When Katie is doing great, he celebrates with me. When she's struggling deeply, he commiserates with me. When I'm a sobbing mess, he lies down on the bed with me and counts breaths, helping me calm down. When I'm thrilled with life, he dances around the kitchen with me and kisses me tenderly on the cheek.

How did I get so lucky?

LAUREN

Winter 2018

I sat quietly at my desk, staring down at my phone in my lap. Apprehensive as I was, I didn't want to miss the call that I knew was coming any minute.

When my phone finally started buzzing, I rose from my chair and waved at my coworkers to let them know I was going to be gone for a little while. Then, as I stepped into the tiny meeting room and shut the lime green door, I answered the call.

"Hi, Lauren! This is Dr. Steve calling from Timberline Knolls for Katie's family therapy session."

"Hi," I replied automatically.

"Hi, Lauren," I heard Katie say. Luckily, she didn't sound angry with me, but my nerves were still severely frayed. After our slight altercation on Christmas, I was worried she would hold a grudge, as she often did.

"Hey, how are you doing?" I answered softly. Before she could respond, my mom suddenly joined the call, her loud, friendly voice breaking into the conversation.

"Hello! Katie, are you there?"

"Yeah, I'm here. Hi, Mom."

"Are we calling Lauren in?"

"Yeah, she's already—"

"Hello!" My dad's voice cut in, and before the chaotic conversation could resume, Katie's psychiatrist spoke up.

"All right, we've got everyone here now! Thank you all for joining this therapy session. I know that Katie was wanting to talk with you all, so it's really nice of you to take time out of your day to make that happen."

"Of course!" exclaimed my mom, sweet and chipper as ever.

"We love you, sweetie," said my dad tenderly. "We're happy to do whatever we need to do to help you get through this."

I remained silent. Of course, I wanted to do everything possible to help Katie. However, I was concerned that this family therapy setup would simply be a means for Katie to say whatever she wanted to me without me being able to defend myself. Plus, I was having to take a lengthy break from my work to make time for the meeting. In general, I was a bit iffy about the situation.

"So, Katie, do you want to start?"

"Uh, sure. So . . . Mom, are you mad at me?"

"What? No! Why would you think that?"

"Well, I hadn't talked to you in a long time, but you never called me to check up on me."

"Oh, Katie," my mom sighed. "I don't like to call you because I don't know your schedule and I never know where you are. I call one lodge, and they direct me somewhere else, and then I get directed somewhere else . . . It's just a lot easier to wait for you to call me."

"But I hadn't called you for a long time."

"I know, sweetheart. I was getting pretty worried about you for a little bit, but I started to think that maybe you weren't calling me because you were doing so well and you just didn't feel the need to talk to me. I was missing you a lot, but I didn't want to interrupt any progress you were making."

"I just . . . I thought you had given up on me." I heard Katie start crying, and I leaned back in my chair, wishing I could hug her and shake her at the same time. *Why is she trying to test Mom like that?* I wondered. *If you want to talk to Mom, just call her! Don't wait around to see how long it takes her to decide to go out of her way to contact you.*

"Oh, sweetheart, I would never give up on you. You know that."

"I didn't know . . ."

"Oh, Katie. I won't do that again, okay? If I don't hear from you in a while, I'll just go ahead and call up there."

"O-okay."

And, of course, Mom is willing to go to ridiculous lengths when Katie could just stop being so stubborn . . .

"Now, Lauren, do you have anything you'd like to talk about?" Dr. Steve asked.

"Oh . . . Me?"

He chuckled. "Yes, you."

"Um, I mean, Katie's the one who invited me here . . ."

"That's fine. We'll have Katie start. What did you want to talk to Lauren about?"

"Well, I just wanted to talk about what happened on Christmas . . ." Katie started hesitantly.

"What part?" I asked.

"Well, when we got into a fight. I could tell you got angry with me, but I wasn't really sure why. And I'm sorry because I know that I didn't react well to it, but . . . That's not really a reflection of how I'm actually doing right now. I wanted to show you all that I've been doing so much better since coming here and prove how much progress I've made. But instead, I just reacted immaturely, and that made me really upset with myself."

"Katie, I definitely noticed a difference in you," I assured her. "I notice it right now! I don't want you to worry about us not being able to tell how much progress you've made because that is more than clear. I was just upset on Christmas because . . . Well, I had asked you how you were doing, and you said you didn't want to talk about that since it was Christmas. It just hurt my feelings because I had driven five hours on Christmas to see you and find out how things were going, and you refused to tell me. I guess I just thought it was pretty selfish."

"Oh, that's not how I perceived it at all," interrupted my dad. "To me, she said that because she didn't want us to have to spend our Christmas just talking about her. I actually thought it was a very selfless thing to say."

"Okay, well, I never talk to Katie, and I really never see her, so I actually wanted to take that opportunity to learn how she was doing," I continued, a little annoyed. "I wanted to know what was working, what wasn't, when she thought she might be home, stuff like that. And it offended me when she denied me that!"

"I understand," acknowledged my mom fairly. "I talk to Katie almost every single day—sometimes more than once a day—so I know everything about how she's doing. But Lauren only gets occasional updates from me, not even from Katie. I can see why she wanted to ask Katie about it and why she might have misinterpreted what Katie said."

"Lauren," Katie broke in. "I'm sorry you thought that's what I was saying. That's not what I meant at all. I just didn't want Christmas to be all about me again. I didn't have a problem with talking to you about everything that had been going on with me."

"I mean, it was already all about you. We had just driven hours away to see you. Our whole day was structured around you."

"I know . . ."

"Look, it's okay," I said gruffly. "I'm sorry I got so upset with you. I see your side of it now. It's not a big deal." At this point, I just wanted to be done with it, put it behind me, and move on. I was hoping Katie felt the same way.

"Well, Lauren, how about I start calling you too?" Katie suggested earnestly. "I can just call you a couple of times a week to update you on how I'm doing. Would you like that?"

"Yes." I smiled. "If you don't mind."

"Great. I'll start doing that."

"Okay, that was a productive conversation!" praised Dr. Steve. "I'm so glad you two could work through that. Now, I also wanted to talk to you all about something else. So, as you know, Katie has a mental illness, and that affects how she perceives herself and how she perceives the world. So, Rob and Anne, I know we've talked about how Katie has a core belief about herself that has been constructed and solidified over the course of her life so far. And that core belief is that she is worthless."

My parents and I made sounds indicating we were about to interrupt, so Dr. Steve raised his voice slightly as he continued. "Now, we all know that to be completely untrue, but that is the inner narrative she has established for herself, and it is going to take a significant amount of time and effort to change that. Something to keep in mind is that, because of this negative core belief, whenever you say something nice about Katie, she doesn't take it seriously. She doesn't think you really believe it because she doesn't believe it about herself."

"So . . ." I swallowed, then tried again. "So, like, when I tell her I love her, she doesn't believe me?"

"No," responded Katie tearfully. "I just think you're saying it because you feel like you have to because you're my sister. Not because you really mean it."

"But I do mean it!"

"This is just part of her mental illness, Lauren."

"Lauren, I don't want you to feel bad about it because it's not your fault at all. It's my own problem to deal with. I'm learning that I can't blame you or Mom and Dad or anyone because of the things my mind makes me believe. I'm trying to take responsibility for all of this and remind myself that it is my mental illness. Like, before, whenever you would say you love me, I would think, *She doesn't really love me.* Now, when I initially have that negative thought, I kind of argue with it and say, *Yes, she does love me.*"

"It's going to take a long time, but if she keeps working on changing her thoughts about herself, her core beliefs about herself will change," Dr. Steve explained patiently.

"We are so proud of you, Katie," said Dad, sounding choked up. My throat was too tight to respond, so I simply nodded as tears wet my face. Obviously, no one could see my affirmative gesture from over the phone, but I hoped they understood.

A few minutes later, after a bit more discussion with Mom and Dad, we ended the family therapy session. I scrubbed over my face with shaking hands, trying to collect myself before I returned to my desk. The session had gone a million times better than I'd imagined. The psychiatrist had been entirely fair and had been just as concerned about me sharing my side as he was about Katie sharing hers. And Katie had been so mature. There was no doubt that she was doing a ton better.

The only thing that kept nagging at the back of my head was the fact that she apparently didn't believe me when I told her I loved her. That just shattered my heart. With a deep breath, I marched back to my seat and resolved to do everything in my power to show Katie that I truly do love her—and always will.

MOM

Winter 2018

I was at home when I got the phone call from Katie.
"Hello?" I answered, then immediately held the phone away from my ear. Katie was clearly yelling at someone, her booming voice blasting through the phone.

"Whoa, whoa, whoa. Who are you talking to?" I asked, feeling sick because this did not sound like a good situation.

"The police!" she snapped. Then, her voice got slightly quieter (or at least more muffled) as she turned her mouth away from the phone. "Get away from me!" I heard her roar. "I'm not going anywhere!"

It took a long time to get the full story, but I was finally able to piece together what had happened. Apparently, Katie had been agitated because some girl in the dining hall had said her laugh was too loud. As a result, Katie had gotten mad and bent her metal knife.

"That's our property," one of the caretakers had chided. "You can't be breaking our property."

This had annoyed Katie, but she'd tried to bend it back, and it had broken. At that point, the caretaker had become alarmed. "What are you thinking right now?" she'd asked. And Katie had snarkily responded, "Well, I'm thinking about going out into the woods with this knife."

Now, Katie has a mental illness. She has thoughts like these all the time, but it doesn't mean she's going to act on them. I know that, and my family knows that, but I understand that in this situation, the caretaker had to act with caution.

Unfortunately, Katie didn't seem willing to cut the caretaker some slack. As she relayed the story over the phone, Katie insisted that she'd only *thought* about going into the woods with the knife. She'd never actually stated she was going to do it.

After lunch, Katie had gone back to Willow and returned to her room since she'd still been aggravated. However, she'd become upset when no one had come and checked on her. I guess she'd felt like she'd asked for help, and it hadn't been given to her. So, she'd snuck out of the lodge behind someone else as they were leaving (the doors are generally locked).

It was a snow-on-the-ground, cold Chicago winter—and Katie wasn't dressed for the weather. And she certainly wasn't in a good frame of mind to be leaving the facility. I have no idea what she was thinking when she decided to just leave.

Luckily, a caretaker had come out right behind her and insisted she come back inside, but Katie had less-than-politely declined.

"If you don't come inside right now, I'm calling a code green," the caretaker had warned. This basically meant that somebody was escaping without being discharged.

"Fine, call a code green," Katie had responded rudely.

So, they did—and the police were called.

At this point, it was clear that Katie wasn't cooperating. I could still hear her saying she wouldn't go with the police even as she was on the phone with me. In fact, I was astounded at how she was speaking to the officers. It was horrible.

"Let me talk to the police," I finally commanded, breaking into her diatribe. Instantly, I heard her shove the phone toward someone.

"Hello," said a deep male voice.

"Hey, what's going on?" I demanded.

"Look, your daughter needs to go to the hospital. Either she'll go willingly, or we're going to arrest her and take her to the police station."

"I can convince her to go with you," I insisted in a pleading tone. The officer didn't seem so sure, but he handed the phone back to Katie.

"Katie. You're gonna have to go with them. Please just cooperate. We'll figure it out, okay? Hopefully you won't be at the hospital that long." Katie grumbled angrily in response. "As soon as I get off the phone, I'm gonna pack and I'll be there right away. How's that sound?"

"Fine," Katie grunted.

I didn't end up going that night because I didn't know if I would be able to see her. Once she was admitted to the hospital in Chicago, it was already pretty late, and I knew I wouldn't get there until eight or nine in the evening. I wouldn't even be able to see her until the next day anyway because visiting hours would be over.

By the next morning, Katie had decided she didn't want me to come up yet. She wanted to wait until she was back at Timberline Knolls for me to visit so we could have more time together. Unfortunately, it took her a long while to get discharged. I worried that she hadn't improved as much as we'd thought—that things weren't getting better.

Trying to hold on to hope, I prayed.

LAUREN

Winter 2018

I was in the car with Jordan when Katie called me, just as she'd promised she would. Ever since our family therapy session, she had been quite diligent in contacting me to update me on her progress. I was so grateful to know more about what was going on, but her timing wasn't always that great—not that it was necessarily her fault. She was only allowed to make phone calls at certain times of the day, and only for so many minutes.

Plus, at this point, she was at the hospital in Chicago thanks to her wild antics that day. Soon after being readmitted to her original lodge and only a few days before she was meant to be picked up and brought home, she had gone rogue and tried to escape the mental facility. I had been rehearsing what I would say to her all day, but my mind went uncomfortably blank as I answered the phone.

"Hello?" I said as Jordan pulled into a parking spot in front of Joey B's.

"Lauren?"

"Hey, Katie. How are you doing? I was hoping to talk to you."

"Did you hear about what's been going on?"

"Yeah." I hesitated to say too much. I was frustrated with Katie for what had occurred the previous day, but I didn't want my feelings to ruin our conversation. I had been doing such a good job of talking to Katie without creating issues lately, and I didn't want to break my streak when she was in such a precarious mental state already.

"I'm so pissed off that I'm in the hospital," Katie exploded, her rage impossible to misunderstand, even over the phone. "They're all liars at TK."

"Katie," I began reproachfully.

"What? Are you seriously going to defend them? Do you really think that I went crazy and ran through the woods with a knife?"

"Katie, Katie. Try to relax for a second. That's not what I'm saying at all. All I'm saying is that you should probably take at least some responsibility for the situation. I mean, if you hadn't broken that knife in the dining hall, then none of this would have happened. You wouldn't be at the hospital right now."

"That girl was being so rude to me. She told me I was laughing too loud. Seriously? You're going to complain because I'm laughing?" She snorted derisively.

"That was really rude of her," I replied soothingly. "She shouldn't have said that. But you shouldn't have reacted the way you did. The people at Timberline Knolls were probably worried about your mental state because of what happened before Christmas . . . with the socks."

"That's so stupid. The nurse asked if I was unsafe, and I said no. Then, she asked if I was thinking about hurting myself with the knife. I said yes because, honestly, I was. But that doesn't mean I had any intention of *actually* hurting myself. That's just what mental illness is—I frequently think of things like that."

"Yes, I totally understand. I just think that probably *she* didn't understand. She heard what you were saying and worried that you were going to actually hurt yourself."

"Whatever. It was stupid."

I sighed. My mom had told me that not long after the episode in the dining hall, Katie had snuck out of her lodge. One of the nurses had followed her and insisted that she go back inside—or else she would call a code green.

"Fine. Call code green," Katie had bit out scathingly.

Apparently, the police had had to come, and Katie had made some biting remarks to the officer in charge. At that point, the officer had called my mom, indicating that Katie was going to the hospital whether she wanted to or not. It was just a matter of whether she would make the decision to go herself or would be forced to go.

My mom had understood his meaning. After pleading on the phone with her for several minutes, my mom had finally succeeded in convincing Katie to go to the hospital. Still, Katie wasn't pleased at all . . . if her attitude so far was any indication.

"Why did you run outside, Katie? I just don't understand what your plan was," I muttered, rubbing my temples as Jordan glanced curiously at me.

"I wanted to leave. I was done being there."

"But how were you planning to get home? There was snow on the ground, and you didn't have any money or means for transportation."

"I was going to walk."

"Katie . . . You hear how irrational that is, don't you?" My voice became shrill with exasperation. "I mean, I completely understand that you wanted to come home, and I want you to come home too, but you would have frozen to death if you had seriously tried to walk home from *Chicago*."

"Hmph."

"Katie, I did want to talk to you about something . . ."

"What?" she responded a touch petulantly.

"I—it's just that I really miss you, and I want you to be able to come home soon. And well . . ."

"What?"

"Look, maybe I'm wrong here, but here's what I think happened. I think that your release date was coming up, and you panicked. You were afraid that you weren't going to be able to keep getting better once you left Timberline Knolls. And I get that, I do, but I need you to come home soon." I gasped quietly as tears streamed down my face. "I miss my sister. It's been so hard being away from you. I just can't stand it if you stay there too much longer. I know it feels safe there, and I know you've been able to make so much progress during your time at TK, but I just know that you can continue to do well at home. Please don't sabotage yourself so that you can stay there. We need you to come home."

Katie started to protest, and I think she was planning on denying all of the things I had just said, but as I started to sob, she softened her voice. "Lauren, I want to come home too. I'll be able to come home soon. I just have a few more things I need to work on here, okay? But I should be able to come home within a couple of weeks. I just wasn't ready yet."

"Okay," I whispered gruffly.

"I'm out of phone time," said Katie regretfully. "I'll talk to you later."

"Okay. I love you, Katie."

"I love you too."

I buried my face in Jordan's shoulder, and we sat there in the parking lot for ten more minutes as my breathing slowed and my face dried.

MOM

Winter 2018

Despite the code green crisis, Katie truly was doing better. Rob and I could both tell that she was using her coping skills regularly and trying to be more aware of her thoughts and emotions.

For example, she was better able to recognize when cognitive distortions were skewing her thinking and influencing her emotions. When things got to be too much, she was consistently practicing strategies like mindfulness, distraction, self-soothing, and even radical acceptance—reminding herself "it is what it is." By this point, she was a pro at identifying and acknowledging her emotions while doing her best to keep those feelings from completely taking over. It was a marked difference from where she had begun months earlier upon entering TK.

Rob and I were thrilled that her time at Timberline Knolls had been so beneficial for her—and, honestly, for us too. The family therapy sessions had given us a lot of tools to better communicate with and help Katie.

Of course, we didn't want her to leave the residential facility before she was at a good enough place in her recovery, but we were ready for her to come home. It had been three months, and we had gone through three major holidays without her—Thanksgiving, Christmas, and New Year's. We missed her so much, and we wanted to go back to spending time as a whole family. (Not to mention, once the new year had started, Rob and I had had to begin paying out of pocket since my insurance plan had started over.)

Finally, I got the news that Katie was being released. I was ecstatic! Lauren was the only one who would be able to go with me, and we planned to pick Katie up that Sunday, a few days before Valentine's Day. My baby was finally coming home.

LAUREN

Winter 2018

Mom and I parked the car in the tiny parking lot near the front office. I danced in my seat, anxious to get out and get Katie. It was finally time to bring her home.

I unbuckled my seat belt and shot out of the car, my feet crunching softly in the snow. Head down, I led the way across the street and to the front door, then let my mom pass in front of me to talk to the receptionists.

"Who are you here for?"

"We're here to pick up Katie."

"Okay! What lodge is she in?"

"Willow."

"All right! Why don't you just look at these forms here, and we will let her know that you've arrived."

Minutes later, we were marching back to our car, smiling in anticipation. After driving across a quaint bridge, we parked directly in front of Willow Lodge, the trunk of the car facing the door. Then, we bounced out of the vehicle and skipped into the entrance of the building.

Unfortunately, our prancing progress was halted there, as the door was locked and we couldn't come all the way inside. So, we waited in that in-between space, shifting from foot to foot, craning our heads to see if Katie was coming.

"I hear her!" my mom exclaimed.

"I can't see her though," I remarked, standing on my tiptoes and turning my head from side to side.

Finally, *finally*, Katie came into sight. She had clearly lost a lot of weight and was holding several bags filled with everything she'd brought and obtained since arriving at Timberline Knolls.

"You're coming home," I breathed as I hugged her fiercely.

"My turn!" My mom nudged me out of the way and wrapped Katie in her arms. "I'm so glad we get to have you back, sweetie."

Katie laughed and grinned and joked around as we each took some of her things and headed back to the car. I could tell she wasn't perfect, but she was so much better than she'd been when my parents had dropped her off. She had made so much progress, and I saw that vibrant life radiating off of her. The whole car ride home, we chatted and listened to music and thanked God for all He had done for our family.

KATIE

Fall 2019

JOURNAL ENTRY

I realized today that people with depression aren't just fighting when they're depressed. They're fighting every single day: the good days, the bad days, and all the days in between.

Today was an average day for me. Nothing too exciting or great about it, though I'm not depressed, so one could say today was just an everyday kind of day. I woke up, got ready, grabbed a granola bar, and left for class. My classes were like they always are—pretty mundane. It wasn't until my drive home that my day turned extraordinary.

I was driving home when I had what one may call an intrusive thought; for no reason, out of the blue, I had a dark (suicidal) thought. Now, it's taken me years to figure it out, but this doesn't mean I'm depressed; it merely means that darkness is trying to get in. Although the thought was there and it bothered me,

I didn't let it control me. I didn't let it take over my feelings or actions. I made the choice to fight against the darkness, a choice that I make frequently and that I believe everyone who has struggled with continuous depression has to make on a somewhat regular basis.

While I believe that fighting or surrendering to the darkness is a choice we all make, I understand that the frequency of how often we must wage that battle differs from person to person and experience to experience. At this point in my life, I encounter the darkness a couple of times a week.

What fighting back looks like for me is internally telling myself "NO." Sometimes, it's a quiet "No," sometimes it's a loud and desperate "No," but either way, I am making the choice to fight. I'm not saying depression is a choice because it's not. But we all get to choose to fight or surrender. I know all too well that, sometimes, surrendering is easier and feels like the only possible option or even the best option . . . but it's not.

Anyway, back to the point. Here is the imagery that went on in my head when I was thinking about this on my way home: depression, or darkness, is like a thick, oily substance trying to seep through the cracks of your heart. I believe that one naturally has a heart filled with an abundance of light and that what causes people to have darkness is experiences. So, the core of you starts off beaming with light, right? And then, something happens, and that once flawless outer layer of your heart becomes cracked. And for every crack, it becomes easier for darkness to slip through. It takes healing for those cracks to close, and even then, it leaves a scar with thinner tissue that allows the darkness to maintain at least a shadow of an effect. This effect may not always be a bad thing. For example, it can protect you from experiencing the same trauma. Either way, some experiences stick with you, but that doesn't mean you have to let it take over your life.

For me, when I was hit by darkness while driving home, instead of letting the thick substance seep through the scarred cracks of my heart, I decided to fight that darkness because I know how extraordinary life is when it's filled with joy, gratitude, and an overwhelming amount of light. So, I fought. And guess what? I won—this time. Sometimes I lose, and the loss may show itself as a bad day, week, or month(s), and sometimes it can turn into full-blown depression. But not today. Today, I chose to fight. Today, I beat the darkness.

LAUREN

Epilogue

Katie wasn't just back. She was *back*. I finally got to see the sister I'd been missing for several years.

Katie wasn't perfect, but she was healing. And she was effectively responding to and coping with her mental illness. Whenever she experienced a strong emotion, she acknowledged it, tried to understand why she was feeling that way, and communicated her needs and insights to us. She was able to look at each of her thoughts, feelings, and interactions in a fairly rational way and push against her negative internal narrative. We were all amazed and impressed by her remarkable progress. She was working so very hard, and it was paying off. For the first time in a long time, I was able to see a happy, meaningful future for her.

Today, six years after returning from Timberline Knolls, Katie is thriving. It took her almost eight years in total, but she worked unbelievably hard to attain her bachelor's degree in education. She was even able to attend Truman University, a few hours away from home, which highlighted how far she had come. We never could have imagined her being apart from my mom and dad. But after learning more about herself and the root of her mental health challenges, she was able to truly blow everyone away with her tenacity to achieve everything she could have dreamed of without letting her mental illness slow her down.

In the last couple of years of her undergraduate experience, she also worked with AmeriCorps as an educator tutoring elementary school kids struggling with math. Her endless capacity for love and compassion made an immediate impression, and she was promptly promoted and given additional responsibilities, which she embraced with open arms and open heart. Before long, she had developed programs related to math and mental health, demonstrating her deep care for her students' minds—both intellectually and emotionally. This is what made her such a remarkable teacher: her determination to connect with the whole child and educate them holistically while promoting their overall well-being. Her students loved her, her coworkers looked up to her, and she effortlessly paved the way for a stellar career in education.

After passing her boards, Katie was instantly offered a teaching position. Actually, she got three different offers because she is such an inspiring and impressive figure in the world of education! As I write this, I proudly reflect on how many lives she has touched, how many students she has made an indelible impression on, even in her few years as a professional educator. She is a favorite among the children at her school, and she makes every effort to let each student know that they are special, they are capable, and they are worthy.

Outside of school and work, Katie continues to pursue happiness and fulfillment. She was able to move into her own apartment and even got a sweet little dog. She is focusing on her relationships, bettering herself, and, of course, sharing her story to help others find hope. That's one of her main goals in life. After all, if Katie can overcome all she's conquered, anyone can. You can. Your loved one can. There's a reason to hold on, to have hope.

Katie may never be freed of her mental illness, but she will always be the intelligent, compassionate, faithful person that she is today. She will always be my sister, and she will always be so very loved by all who know her. That support, along with Katie's keen determination to beat her mental illness, will see her through. Though she will undoubtedly have many low moments throughout the rest of her days—perhaps lower moments than the average person has to endure—she still has a chance at a happy and fruitful life. After all, mental illness doesn't equal incapacity.

Since the start of her mental health journey, Katie has felt like a butterfly stuck in a bell jar, fluttering around hopelessly, beating her fragile wings against the immovable walls of her mental illness. A delicate little thing, she saw her mental illness as a glass barrier—a prison that held her captive and showcased her worst moments to the rest of the world.

But as we've learned as a family, Katie isn't dainty and defenseless. She is strong and capable and resilient. Any obstacle that bars her path can be overcome with the help of her friends, her family, and herself—as long as she can find the confidence and faith. She isn't enclosed in a humiliating shell that holds her hostage and exposes her to the world's ridicule and damnation. She has power over her own destiny.

Katie is a vibrant and bright beauty, capable of anything as long as she fights for it. As I watch her fight for her mental health every day, I know that her life is hers. And her mental illness can't take that away from her.

ACKNOWLEDGMENTS

Marian and Gena: I cannot thank you enough for endorsing *Bell Jar Butterfly*. You are both such important leaders in the mental health space, and I aspire to make as much of a positive impact in my community as you both do.

Betsy: Thank heavens we were brought together by fate and mutual career goals seven years ago. You quickly went from being my colleague to being my dear friend. As much as I appreciate your willingness to edit this manuscript to get it ready for publication, I most value your friendship, wisdom, and infinitely kind heart.

Savannah: It's wild to think that one of the people I look up to most in this world is someone I have never met in real life! I am so glad that Ballast Books connected us from across the country. You are truly my soul sister in so many ways, but I must admit that you're infinitely more talented than me. Thank you for lending your unique gifts to help me create a compelling cover design that somehow perfectly captures the message and emotion behind *Bell Jar Butterfly*.

Cris: When I think of you, I think of stories. That's one of my favorite things about you and your family—you're storytellers. I love hearing the same ones over and over again and feeling like I was there, even when I wasn't. Thank you for sharing your stories with me and for taking the time to immerse yourself in my family's story. Your feedback helped give me the confidence to get this book out into the world.

Mom: Is there a better mom than you? I certainly don't think so. While no one is perfect, you're the most perfect person I can imagine. There is no one more selfless, more giving, more motivated by unconditional love than you. I hope I can model that strength of heart for my family. Thank you for all you have done for me—for this book and the millions of other things you do every single day.

Dad: Remember when I decided I didn't want to study English? I thought I should pursue a more practical career path. How could I guarantee a secure future for myself and my family as a writer? There's no doubt that you pushed me in the right direction—onto the path that allowed me to apply my gifts, pursue my dreams, and contribute meaningfully to society. Without your push, I wouldn't be publishing this book right now. Becoming an author would be a dream left forever unrealized. Thank you for recognizing what I'm capable of even when I can't see it myself.

My dear sisters: There's nothing like growing up together. Siblings share a bond that can't be matched by any other relationship. After all, who has been there learning and hurting and celebrating and loving along with me for as long as I can remember? My sisters. Through the seasons when we're close and the seasons when we've grown apart, we will always have that unshakable bond. That's one of the reasons why this book is so powerful—it has pieces of all of us in there. And that means it has the capacity to help as many people as possible.

Jordan: Honestly, I don't know how to articulate the impact you've made on me—on the way I communicate, the way I process my feelings, the way I perceive and interact with the world. There is no doubt that I am a better person now than I was ten years ago because of you. I love you more than anything.

Annesley: My precious girl. All I hope for in this life is that you live a happy and healthy life and that you make a positive difference in the world. This book is your mama's effort to make a positive difference. May you do a hundred times better than me in every single regard. You are my whole world.